Mary Chubb was bo.. ... .
joined the staff of the Egypt Exploration Society
in London as an under secretary, and two years
later was sent out to dig at Tell el Amarna – an
experience which inspired a lifelong, if unschol-
arly, enthusiasm for archaeology in general and
Egyptology in particular. Egypt was followed in
1933 with a season in Iraq, at the site of Tell
Asmar, with the Oriental Institute of the
University of Chicago, and a short spell in the
United States.

Mary Chubb first turned her hand to writing and broadcasting in the 1940s, contributing
to *Punch* and working with the BBC. *Nefertiti
Lived Here* first appeared in 1954, followed by
City in the Sand, a colourful account of her experiences of dig life in Iraq.

NEFERTITI

Lived Here

*Mary Chubb in the courtyard of the dig house
at Tell el Amarna*

NEFERTITI
Lived Here

by Mary Chubb

With illustrations by Ralph Lavers

Introduction by Peter Lacovara

LIBRI

First published in 1954. This edition published by Libri Publications
Limited in 1998. Reprinted 2001

© Mary A. Chubb 1954 and 1998

Introduction © Peter Lacovara 1998

ISBN 1-901965-01-5

*Front cover: Painted limestone head of Nefertiti, from Tell el
Amarna. Ägyptisches Museum, Berlin. Inv. no. 21300.
Photo: Margarete Büsing*

*Back cover: John Pendlebury posing in an ancient Egyptian
faience collar*

All rights reserved. No part of this publication may be
reproduced, stored in a retrieval system, or transmitted, in any form
or by any means, electronic, mechanical, photocopying or otherwise,
without the prior written permission of the copyright owners

Exclusive distribution outside North America by
I. B. Tauris and Co. Ltd, 6 Salem Road, London W2 4BU

Designed and typeset by Libri Publications Limited
Printed and bound in Great Britain by Biddles Limited of Guildford

Libri Publications Limited
Suite 296, 37 Store Street
Bloomsbury
London, WC1E 7QF

For Lorna with love

Introduction

MOST archaeological reports are as dry as dust and there are lamentably few accounts able to flesh out their bare bones. One of the best memoirs of excavation life, Mary Chubb's *Nefertiti Lived Here* is uniquely engaging and of interest to everyone from the novice to the scholar. The setting for her recollections, the site of Tell el Amarna, holds endless fascination to all those interested in the field of Egyptology. The ephemeral capital of the 'heretic' pharaoh Akhenaten and his beautiful wife Nefertiti, el Amarna was also the boyhood home of Tutankhamun and the stage on which some of the most momentous events in Egyptian history took place.

Having proscribed the worship of the traditional pantheon, the king who began his reign as Amenhotep IV soon changed his name to Akhenaten, 'the spirit of the Aten', and promulgated a new, monotheistic religion with the Aten as the one god and himself as the divinity's sole representative on earth. Tell el Amarna, 200 miles north of the Theban heartland, was the site chosen for the new capital, Akhetaten, 'The horizon of the Aten'. Conceived as a showplace for the cult of the Aten and the radical new art-style created for it, the city was built on virgin desert ground bordering the Nile in the remote region of Middle Egypt. Akhenaten's architects had seen how the local topography might be employed to enhance the symbolism of the setting, positioning the main royal palaces and temples at the midpoint of a large semicircle described by sheer limestone cliffs.

The site of Tell el Amarna stretches for about eight miles and is about three miles wide at its midpoint, and may have served as home to 20,000 or more individuals in its heyday. It is the best-known town site to survive from ancient Egypt. Clusters of houses, large and small, were located to the north and south of the central city, along with planned housing for the workmen engaged on the construction projects and offices for the diplomatic corps and the bureaucracy associated with the royal court. At the periphery of the site, cut into the forbidding cliffs, were the tombs of the king, his family and most trusted courtiers. The city appears to have been inhabited for only about fourteen years, up to the death of Akhenaten; soon after, the site was abandoned and the former capital and old religion re-instated by the 'boy-king' Tutankhamun. Afterward, the 'Amarna period' was deleted from the official history books and forgotten.

Although the tombs were noted by early travellers and later recorded,[1] no attention was paid to the town itself until 1887, when a farmer's wife digging in the city ruins discovered the famous 'Tell el Amarna Tablets,' diplomatic documents written on clay detailing Egypt's relations with the empires of the ancient Near East. Thereafter, the site was the focus of a number of archaeological field seasons, initial investigations carried out by the Egyptian Antiquities Service being followed up by the great Flinders Petrie, who made the first detailed record of the palaces and temples in the central city in 1891-2.[2]

The Deutsche Orient-Gesellschaft began work at the site in 1907 and concentrated on the clearing of hundreds of houses spread out to the north and south of the central city.[3] The most important of these was that belonging to the sculptor Thutmose, in whose workshop was discovered the famous painted limestone bust of Queen Nefertiti. With the First World War, the German mission's work at the site came to an end and permission to excavate was again given to a British team in 1921 under T.E. Peet and Leonard Woolley.[4]

Work was continued at the site after Peet's death by Henri Frankfort[5] and later by John Pendlebury from 1930 to 1936.[6] In comparing Pendlebury's reports with those of earlier seasons, the organisation and clarity that Mary Chubb brought to the expedition's records are obvious. Indeed, both with the *City of Akhenaten* volumes, and later with the Oriental Institute Expedition in Iraq, Miss Chubb contributed much to the setting of new standards in archaeological publication.

Work at Amarna ceased with the Second World War and Pendlebury's untimely death, but was resumed in 1976, again by a team from the Egypt Exploration Society in London.[7] The ongoing excavations, directed by Barry J. Kemp, are a model of archaeological reporting, and are adding much to our knowledge of the site and this pivotal period in Egyptian history.

Interested readers might like to note that, in addition to Mary Chubb's account, J.D.S. Pendlebury himself penned a popular book on the excavations entitled *Tell el-Amarna* (London, 1935), while Sir Leonard Woolley recounts his work at the site in the autobiographical *Spadework* (London, 1953).

Peter Lacovara,
Boston, 1998.

[1] See for example, Norman de Garis Davies, *The Rock Tombs of El Amarna*, I (London, 1903).

[2] W.M.F. Petrie, *Tell el Amarna* (London, 1894). For an account of Petrie's work at the site, see also Margaret S. Drower, *Flinders Petrie: A Life in Archaeology* (London, 1985), pp. 189-97.

[3] Ludwig Borchardt, 'Excavations at Tell el-Amarna, Egypt in 1913-1914,' *The Smithsonian Report for 1915* (1921), pp. 445-57.

[4] Charles Leonard Woolley and Thomas Eric Peet, *The City of Akhenaten*, I (London, 1923).

[5] Henri Frankfort, 'Preliminary Report on the Excavations at Tell El-'Amarnah, 1928-9,' *Journal of Egyptian Archaeology* 15 (1932), pp. 143-49.

[6] Henri Frankfort and J.D.S. Pendlebury, *The City of Akhenaten*, II (London, 1933).

J.D.S. Pendlebury, 'Preliminary Report on the Excavations at Tell El-'Amarna, 1930-1931,' *Journal of Egyptian Archaeology* 17 (1931), pp. 233-44.
——————— 'Summary Report on the Excavations at Tell El-'Amarna, 1935-1936,' *Journal of Egyptian Archaeology* 22 (1936), pp. 192-98.
——————— *The City of Akhenaten,* III (London, 1951).

[7] B.J. Kemp, 'The Window of Appearance at El-Amarna, and the Basic Structure of this City,' *Journal of Egyptian Archaeology* 62 (1976), pp. 81-99.
——————— 'The City of el-Amarna as a source for the study of urban archaeology in ancient Egypt.' *World Archaeology* 9 (1977), pp. 123-39.
——————— *Amarna Reports* I- (London, 1984-).

DRAMATIS PERSONAE

Hilary: *Hilary W. Waddington, architect*
John: *John Devitt Stringfellow Pendlebury,*
                        field director
Ralph: *Ralph S. Lavers, architect*
Tommy: *Herbert Walter Fairman, epigraphist*

Chapter One

THE top of the packing-case slid heavily to the ground, and along with it went my heart. If anyone can tell me of a sadder place to be sad in than the basement of a teetering Bloomsbury mansion on a wet February morning, I should hate to hear about it.

Unaware of the uncomfortable edge of the packing-case on which I now seated myself, and turning away from the rolls of musty paper inside it which I had been told to look through, I stared out of the small, grimy window into the area outside.

Above, rain fell out of a foggy whiteness, splashing up from the invisible pavement against the hurrying, shapeless legs which slip-slopped across my line of vision; rain trickled down the area railings; rain, I knew, would make the coming lunch-hour less of a release than usual; for the normal atmosphere of the steamy, cheap little restaurant I usually went to, with its wafts of cabbage and cheese and fish, would be enriched today by a kind of sustained ground bass of wet mackintosh.

This Bloomsbury basement was the store-room of a learned Society which sent out expeditions to excavate in Egypt, later giving the results of these excavations in a series of leisurely and dignified publications. Upstairs, the Society's committee room and office occupied the whole of the first floor of the house, once a stately Victorian drawing-room. The office was in front, looking out above the tops of the buses, sliding between the plane trees, to the grass of a London Square and the solid line of well-proportioned houses on the western side. Behind the office was the committee room, very large and fine, reached through a great double door, its far end nearly all window, the side walls almost hidden by the extensive

7

Library, and by tall cabinets of files holding hundreds of photographs and lantern slides.

Down here, where I sat grousing, the shades of little Victorian boot-boys and kitchen-maids seemed to be scurrying about in the shadowy old kitchen behind me. Where once great roaring fires had glowed in the range, and the kitchen staff had toiled to put perfection into a meal to be subsequently hauled up a steep and twisting flight of stairs, all was rust and dust and melancholy quiet. The old range was piled high with wooden boxes full of the Society's publications and annual reports. On the dresser opposite, where lustrous dishes and plates and sauceboats had glowed in the firelight, there now stood row upon row of square brown paper parcels, thick with dust, their once white labels almost as dark. 'Oxyrhynchus Papyri' one could make out dimly if one gazed up at the top shelf. 'New Sayings of Jesus and Fragments of a Lost Gospel' now held the place of honour once dominated by an outsize soup-tureen. The dresser drawers, no longer repositories for teacloths and silver-polish, and an occasional hastily concealed saucy note from the milkman to the under-housemaid, suggesting the Holborn Empire for next Saturday evening, were now crammed to bursting with scraps of Egyptian pottery and beads and discarded photographs, bits of cameras and surveying instruments, notebooks and maps, the junk of many an expedition.

I had arrived in this job a year before, my head full of newly acquired shorthand curlywiggles and the thought of my luck at landing as a first post the assistant secretaryship of this Society. Up till then the whole work of the office had been in the hands of one secretary, a good kind soul who had taken on the job in the days when a ladylike visit to the office between the hours of 10 and 4 had been more than enough to keep pace with the work of the Society. The membership had been small, the committee elderly and courtly; a staid expedition occasionally set out for a winter's work in Egypt, and came quietly back again in the spring with very little fuss, to lay the results before the secretary and committee. But times were very different now between the wars. In 1923 the tomb of Tutankhamun had been discovered, and things were never the same again. Excavations in Egypt suddenly became front-page news, and the membership of this particular Society rocketed up with the additional names of hundreds of people —some of them, true enough, genuinely interested in Egyptology for the first time, whose interest was to remain alive; but many superficially intrigued by the passing excitement of the great discovery, their imaginations fired by the sudden dramatic emphasis on the material details of a young life which had ended more than three thousand years before. Everyone was familiar with the somehow pathetic relics appearing in every illustrated paper—the gauntlets, the walking-sticks, the hunting-gear.

This peak membership held for a short time, then slowly began to sink back as the excitement abated, and the scatter-brains whose eyes had popped at the coloured pictures of so much gold and jewellery began to wonder if they could really spare two guineas' worth of annual subscription to a learned Society any longer. But even though the membership began to drop, the boom had its lasting effect in the increased amount of the Society's work, and a general sense of speeding-up. The committee became larger, and younger and perhaps more forceful men sat round the table and urged the need for more far-reaching excavation. By the early thirties the subscriptions were steadily, if slowly dropping, but the expeditions were increasing and needed more and more money. How to get it? The secretary was getting older, yet the office needed far longer than the 10 to 4 routine if she was to keep up with the mass of new work. The young men flustered her; they came home and shied their results and their accounts and their photographs

9

into the office, and then retired to write up their publications, expecting that she would in the meantime reduce all the non-scholastic side of their work to apple-pie order without having to bother them with any further questions. It dawned slowly on the committee that she needed help; it was agreed that in spite of the precarious financial position an Assistant Secretary should be added to the party—and I got the job.

When I arrived for the first day's work I think I must have held the record for knowing less about Egyptology than any other person who had ever crossed that learned threshold, with the possible exception of Mrs. Wilk, whom I met that day very unexpectedly, stern end on, and subsequently, although not so unexpectedly, every day. Then, as always, she was on all fours, moving slowly backwards, towing bucket and mop after her, and had just reached the doorway as I arrived. Then, as always, working round her with difficulty, I said, "Terribly sorry to step on your nice clean floor," and she would answer invariably, "'S all ri', ducks." Her face remains a blank.

My ignorance didn't matter in my junior position. There was not the remotest likelihood of a junior member of the London office actually going to Egypt, and there was little about the office itself to stir up a wish in anyone to do so. There were some pleasant but unexciting water-colours of the Nile hanging round the walls of the office; and the excavation photographs were so many, and in many cases so amateurish in execution, flat and grey with under-exposure, some of them even patchy with bad developing, that they might have damped one who had come to work there full of enthusiasm for the subject, which I certainly had not.

All I had really wanted was a job—any job so long as it would keep me—so that I could go to an art school in the evenings and study sculpture. I thought that however dull a job might be by day it wouldn't matter if it was the means whereby I could find myself every evening climbing the four flights of stone stairs to the door marked 'Sculpture and Modelling' in the Central School of Arts and Crafts in Kingsway. But I was wrong; after a year in my learned Society, heedless of what it might have taught me, I was sitting on the edge of a packing-case in a dingy basement, aware that I was through. I couldn't go on like this any more.

The whole trouble lay in the fact that the kind lady boss hadn't the faintest idea of how to get any work out of me. From the moment when we first faced each other, giggling nervously, across the office table, she silver-haired, tall, yet diffident, I an uneasy combination of ignorance and cheek, we somehow failed to work together. She was overburdened, and we both knew it; but she would never pass on to me anything to do that would really have helped her. I never could guess if this sprang from some deep, possibly quite unconscious fear of what might happen if I became really knowledgeable about the work—or if she simply thought I was unequal to it. The result was that she still went on wrestling with a growing tangled heap of difficult administrative work, while I dawdled about on the fringe, wasting my time with work which could easily have been done by a near-moron of an office boy. I had come prepared at least to work hard and earn my pay—I wonder what the typist of today, holding down a minimum £5 a week job without necessarily being able to spell, would think of my £3 3s. 0d. less insurance? But the only thing that hurt my pride then about my wages was that they came out of the petty cash.

The fault was on my side to the extent that I did not exactly beg my chief to give me more work to do. If I had begun my work there, intent on getting to know something about Egyptology, everything might have been different. But there we were—the Secretary either would not, or could not, hand over any responsible jobs to me; and my initial good intentions faded quietly away, my faculties went flabby, and I began to do even my office-boy jobs badly and with difficulty, for I was inevitably and desperately bored.

So here I was, on a cold and rainy morning, in the gloomy basement, wondering what my next move should be. How much longer could I stick it? Ought I to stick it? How could I find a new job while I was still in this one? How could I explain why I wanted to leave, even though I felt sure that the news would be received with something like relief upstairs? I must think it over when I got back to my room, not now in this miserable basement. I got up; and the faint rustle of my little below-stairs companions seemed to stir round me again before the shadows engulfed them. Did I hear the faint echo of a sniff as they went? Would it be sympathy, or Cockney derision for one who didn't know when she was lucky? "*Garn*—three pun' a week, an' yer work done by arps-five"— and they were gone, with a wave of a pipe-stem arm lost in a ghostly boot, and the flicker of a grubby print frock, into the depths of the kitchen.

What had I been sent down to find, Heaven knows how long ago? I stood and thought. The big case in the little front room. I was to look through the contents for a painting from a Theban tomb which was wanted for some publication or other.

The lid was already off. I pulled out roll after roll of gritty, grimy cartridge paper. The strength with which each resisted every effort to haul it flat testified to the length of time it had lain undisturbed. Most of them had several sheets rolled up together, and these sprang loose infuriatingly at unexpected moments. I took them all into the depths of the old kitchen beyond, switched on the one dim electric light, and found a few heavy books to hold down the edges of the snapping, crackling, exasperating rolls. After a long time I found the painting, last but one. I rolled up the other drawings and carted them back to the case. It was not quite empty—there was something hard lying on the wooden floor.

I hung over the case, and unwound the dusty cloth round the stony-feeling core. When it was freed I could see a smooth hard surface, and could dimly make out a dull grey pattern. I rubbed it idly with a finger—and then stood staring. I felt the same exquisite shock that comes when you suddenly find a hedgesparrow's nest. You part the leaves of a dingy old ivy stump in a shady copse—nothing here but grey-green leaves and blackened wood—perhaps a little lower; surely you saw her fly off from this very stump. But there is still nothing. And then you lift one more leaf—and there it is—with four eggs. That unearthly, silken, summer blue, faintly luminous in the neat dark cradle in that crumbling hollow—just as this unbelievable thing of colour was shining up at me now. I picked it up and carried it under the light; the greyness was thick dust, and I wiped it off carefully. It was a piece of a glazed tile—that was all—but at that blank, bleak moment of depression, it touched off some unguessed spring. The background was an incredible, adorable, hedgesparrow blue, the glazing just high enough to give it the same shell-like glowing quality. Against this grew three lotus flowers; the slender curling stems just firm enough to hold up the swaying heads of the flowers, faintly lilac-tipped within their dream-green, fanshaped sepals.

When I turned it over, a trickle of fine yellow sand slipped through my fingers out of the cracks and crevices of the rough surface beneath. Egyptian sand. I was holding something that had scarcely been touched since it had been found in Egypt years before, something which might still bear the fingerprints not only of the finder, but even of the maker. All the photographs of exquisite jewellery and sculpture which I knew so well upstairs, all the highly cleaned antiquities, sterile behind their glass in the museums, had never moved me as did this small, rough-edged, uncleaned, enchanting thing in my hand.

Suddenly I was invaded by a great longing; I wanted to

know all I could about the place where the tile had come from —what kind of man had made it, what things he saw when he looked up from his work. I just knew enough of the way the tile had been designed to be fairly sure that I knew the name of that place—Tell el Amarna—where even now one of our expeditions was at work. Tell el Amarna; up till this moment a name meaning for me no more than that of a heap of ruins somewhere on the eastern bank of the Nile, where once Tutankhamun had lived, and, yes, Nefertiti—I was clear about her—and her strange husband the Pharaoh Amenhotep IV, whose other curious name was Akhenaten. For the rest, I really knew only two things about it—the information culled from the wildly-typed reports that periodically burst upon our peace from this year's Field Director; reports accompanied by photographs of excavated houses which to the uninitiated all looked very much alike, even to the point of having been taken in a dust storm and developed in a plateful of soup.

And then there were the accounts—usually flung together at the end of the season by some overworked Field Assistant with no head for figures at the best of times, and exasperated at the need to turn his thoughts from his real work to keep them at all. The contents of the accounts envelope would shoot across the office table—a heap of weird scraps of paper from which we at home had somehow to piece together the financial position of the expedition. Here would be an invoice written entirely in Arabic—very pretty, but meaningless to us—the receipt consisting of a thumb-mark pressed on to the paper in purple ink. Further down in the heap, perhaps, a long list of Egyptian names with a sum of money against each—the whole carefully added up, but without a clue as to its significance. The final balance sheet usually had a column touchingly entitled 'Various and Unforeseen'—and contained by the end of the season much of the total funds. Getting our expedition accounts past the auditors was a breathless and hair-raising

14

pastime—never a dull moment. For the rest I knew at that date absolutely nothing either about the place of Tell el Amarna in Egyptian history, or the significance of its excavation.

I looked down at the tile again—the three lotus flowers seemed to sway in a soft breeze; to open slowly to a heavenly day of warm sun and deep blue sky. A shutter in the mind that till then had separated my living self from everything I had heard about ancient Egypt, lifted quite suddenly and quietly. While I still watched the formal static beauty of the tile, somewhere behind my eyes I was aware for the first time of ancient Egypt as a living reality, and I knew that even if I learned much about it I should never be really nearer to it than at this moment.

Somewhere in Egypt at this moment the men whose gear I had helped to pack up in the autumn, and whose enthusiasm for their coming winter's work I had watched with such cool incomprehension, were urgently working, driven by some compulsion, no matter what, which I now perfectly understood. I don't suppose any one of them would have said, "I saw a beautiful thing made by an ancient Egyptian, and that was enough for me to decide on this for a profession." But something, some accidental chance even, had once set that self-same nerve thrumming, so that there was nothing for him to do but go back in space and time and search patiently for the truth.

I laid the tile fragment back, turned off the dim light, and felt my way up the stairs. The fanlight over the front door revealed a darker sky than when I'd come down, with wet dark snowflakes scudding past. But for me the day had lost its gloom; and I ran up the fine carpeted flight to the office, and handed over the painting to the secretary. She said in her kind way: "You've been rather a time, but I expect it was difficult to find. Look what's just come by the post."

It was the latest report from Tell el Amarna, and I was told to sit down at once and type a fresh copy of it, so that no one

15

besides ourselves would have to suffer. As usual the Field Director's typing had its characteristic air of having been done while going over rough country on camel-back. It was long, and it was difficult going, and began with a description of the clearing of several houses. Then came a list of objects. The first was a description of a necklace, beginning:—

Nekclace offaience⁷⁄₈, consis tingof "2POlychrome end)pieces in the shape of?xxx lotus-fowlers.

I sorted it out slowly, and finally produced the following enchanting information about the new find. It had six rows of different designs in faience, and these were:

1 row of small cornflowers in blue and green.
1 row of poppy leaves.
1 row of bunches of grapes in blue.
1 row of white flower petals with yellow base, and 'long corn-flowers', blue on a green stem.
1 row of dates: 2 red, 1 green, 2 blue, 1 green, 2 red, etc.
1 row of lotus petals with blue tips.

Lotus petals with blue tips—I stopped typing and looked across the table at the secretary. The room was very quiet. I took a deep breath.

"No Field Director ought to have to waste time typing out these reports."

"Nor doing accounts," she answered. "Look at this." She held up some pencil calculations straggling obliquely across a page torn out of a diary. We both laughed.

"Wouldn't it be wonderful," I began again, "if one member of each dig did nothing but this sort of work—all the office work which obviously *has* to be done on a dig, but which is an entire waste of time for the Egyptologists themselves to have to stop and do?"

"Make it much easier at this end, as well," said the secretary, gazing hopelessly at a long statement in Arabic, which she was holding upside-down. "But there's no money for extra staff."

FIELD REPORTS

"They might send someone who was on the staff already."
She looked up at me then.

"Send someone who was already—what *do* you mean?"

"I just thought—suppose I—someone—were to go out with
the expedition to Tell el Amarna; he—or she—would come
back with all the details we want for this office—reports,
accounts, photo files, object files—everything—already in good
order, and better still, knowing all about the dig at first hand.
It would save any amount of time out there, and any amount
of time back here. Everybody would gain all round."

I could see a look in her eyes as of one who scarcely dares
believe that the dawn is at hand. For once I seemed to have said
something sensible. Here was a chance—I could see her thinking—a remote one, but still a chance—for her to regain her
treasured solitude for much of the year, and yet have some of
her work alleviated at its very source.

"I wonder what the committee would think," she said
slowly.

Chapter Two

THE committee thought until October, and then suddenly decided that it was a good idea. A new expedition was going out to Tell el Amarna in November, and I was enrolled as secretary to the Field Director. How neatly defined it sounds—evoking a Hollywood vision of a slim figure in cool white, every shining hair in place, typing peacefully in a cool office, while bronzed and sweating Egyptologists are rushing about in the dust and heat.

But this isn't a story from Hollywood. It is a true story, where the secretary, neither slim nor *soignée*, got her fair whack of dust and heat, and might have quailed if she could have foreseen that her official duties would have to be scrambled through, in the short uncertain intervals which might or might not crop up during the daily round between the other unlooked-for jobs, which came to include those of plasterer, chemist, sicknurse, draughtsman, painter, excavator, antiquity-cleaner, carpenter and above all—diplomat. . . .

But of all this I knew nothing and cared less on that misty October evening when I was told that I was to go out with the Tell el Amarna expedition the following month.

My feelings were unexpectedly mixed as I shut the frontdoor behind me, much later than usual, and turned south towards the School of Arts and Crafts. It was now months since that first wild longing to get to Egypt somehow—no matter how—had broken loose in me; remaining a very real thing while its fulfilment seemed impossible. Now that it had suddenly become an established fact that I was on the staff of an expedition, the practical side of things began to loom rather ominously. For one thing I knew none of the others on the field-staff, because there was to be a new Field Director who was at the moment choosing a new staff. The Field Director of the year before and his architect, both of whom I knew fairly well, had resigned during the summer, and were off to a new American expedition in Iraq. That meant that I would begin work in a remote part of Egypt among a very small group of people—six at most, probably—whose faces I would hardly know, let alone the minds behind those faces. Yet I can't say that's much of a drawback, I thought, as I went on my way, kicking my feet through the brittle plane tree leaves already lying thick on the pavement; I like people, and almost more I like the feeling of discovery when unexpected bits of them come up to the surface as they let you get to know them. But to leave Bloomsbury in the late autumn, when it is at its best—I felt homesick already. When your earliest recollections include the surprise of a morning sun the colour of a blood-orange, an unwinking disk looming through a November fog; and another, a little later, of riding down a golden Guilford Street in a wheelbarrow, your mushroom hat nearly submerged below the nodding splendour of potted geraniums for bedding-out, with their strange sharp warm scent nearly stifling you in the May sunshine, while your very greatest friend, the gardener of Brunswick Square, in bashed straw boater and baize apron, trundles you along; when you have these memories somewhere impressed deep down inside you, Bloomsbury even at its nastiest can pull very insistently.

These slight obstacles were nothing, however, when compared with the one which now occurred to me with full force, as I came to Russell Square. The lights had just come on, and the grey twilight sky suddenly changed to deep purple above the brown and gold of the dusty lamplit trees. At the bottom of Southampton Row I could see the lights beginning to shine in the windows of the Central School. I should have to give up my modelling classes. The term there began in October and went on till June, so that I should miss more than half the year's work. Only the week before I had begun work on a half-life-size figure of a girl, and by the time I came back from Egypt there would certainly be a different model and a different pose, so that there was no point now in going on with it. I wondered how Alfred Turner, the head of the Sculpture Department, would take my news. During the previous year, he had sometimes made not entirely discouraging noises when criticizing my work.

I came to Theobald's Road (Tibble's Road to us natives of Bloomsbury), waited for a rabbit tram to dive into its Kingsway warren, and then crossed over. In front of me a young woman with an ungainly step was hurrying along, dull little hat over her ears, dull brown coat above wrinkled stockings. We went up the outer steps of the school together, and then I recognized her, hardly able to believe it, as the model who was posing for the life-class this term. Here, she was indistinguishable from the drab crowds scurrying from their jobs to their little homes; but yet I knew that here, hopelessly concealed by nondescript clothes and bundling gait, was a perfect body, which when poised and still on the model's throne, could scarcely have been surpassed in its fine proportions and sturdy yet delicate lines. How many of these pale men and women, hunched in their shapeless black and grey and brown as they streamed along the pavement behind us, might not be hiding just such unguessed beauty? Suddenly I knew how thankful I was to be getting away from here, where everyone was too busy and too tired to stand up straight and wear jolly-coloured clothes.

I went up to the top floor and took the mackintosh off the roughed-in clay figure on the modelling stand. This was the best moment for self-criticism, at the very first glance, before the eye had become accustomed to some structural fault. I stood back and looked at it—only roughed-in, as yet, but I

20

had a strong feeling that there was already a springiness, a tough liveliness about it, that my earlier jobs had lacked.

"That's a good start," said Alfred Turner quietly, behind me. I turned round, feeling miserable. Now I was certain that I was a fool to be going to Egypt. All these contradictory emotions were really very baffling. But Mr. Turner helped to settle things. I explained the situation while he sat on the edge of a closed clay-bin and gazed at me with his expressive and melancholy eyes. He was a brown-faced man with a silver wing of hair leaning perpetually across his forehead; he always wore a butterfly-collar, several sizes too large, above a broad and slightly sideways bow-tie. Soft-voiced, with an odd trick of mispronouncing a final 'th'.

When I had told him my plans I waited, expecting at best polite indifference.

"You've got hold of life with bofe hands," he said at last,

"and your modellin' won't hurt. You know enough now to go on modellin' in your mind—and you'll quite likely be better after you come back even if you don't touch a piece of clay for months. Look at all the sculpture you can out there—and places, *and* people. Wish *I* could see some Egyptian sculpture in its own place—not always in museums. Yes, you've got hold of life with bofe hands."

Then he said that if I worked all out for the three weeks which remained to me in England—two hours for four evenings a week would mean twenty-four hours of solid modelling—and got on far enough to make it worth while, he would have the job cast for me after I had gone. I turned back to the modelling-stand, and worked in a frenzy until 9.30. Then the model climbed down from the throne, the concentrated silence of the students broke up, everybody began damping cloths and wrapping up their work, and I suddenly realized that I hadn't eaten anything for over eight hours.

What a day. I wanted to get back to my room and its complete quiet. There is nothing like the depths of London—if you choose well—for night silence deeper than anything in the country. I cut past the Red Lion Restaurant, with its coloured lampshades still glowing like jewels through the uncurtained windows; up across Tibble's Road again, up Devonshire Street, through a tiny passage at the north of Queen's Square, and so came, by way of a lane behind the Russell Hotel, into Marchmont Street. Past the house where Shelley, shaking with laughter in the moonlight, once begged his friend to let him in 'for I have been sent down for being an atheist'.

The cleaners had not yet begun their night's work, and pavement and gutters were still littered with the sweepings from all the little shuttered shops—crumpled newspapers, cabbage leaves, onion skins, straw. I turned into a delicatessen store on the corner, a comfortable place which never shut till after midnight, run by a brother and sister with round white faces above their round white aprons. The place was always brilliantly clean, and flung far beyond its doors its welcoming aroma—a strange compound of cheese and spices and pickles and sawdust. With new customers they played Continental: "A leetle R-russian salad for Madam, yes?" As friendly relations were established however, they would gradually give it up, and to everybody's satisfaction, themselves probably not least, revert to type; so that tonight I, a customer of a year's standing, was greeted comfortingly with "'Ullo, dearie, wot's for you?"

Hungry and festive, I bought ham, tongue, salad in mayonnaise, butter, cream cheese and a new French loaf. At last I found myself on the dim top floor of the house in Cartwright Gardens where I had a small back-room. Lights gleamed under doors, but I gained my room unnoticed. For once none of the other inmates—most of them older than I, and much more hardworking—came clattering cheerfully along the shabby passage, with supper-tray or kettle, only too ready to indulge in an interminable chat on the day's doings. I reached the small haven of my room, spread out my splendid and unwise supper —it was now about 11—and wondered how I should ever be ready to leave England in three weeks.

The wheels of the boat-train were keeping time beautifully with the old music-hall song which came into my head when, three weeks later, partly panic-stricken and partly exhilarated, I watched the suburbs of South London beginning to thin out into the fields of Kent: 'Why did I *leave* my little back-*room* in Blooms-ber-*ree*?'

Chapter Three

THE boat heaved, shook from one end to the other, sighed in a dispirited sort of way, and then lay down sideways for a nice rest on the broad bosom of the Mediterranean. Would she never right herself? Slowly she grumbled awake again, trembled, staggered to an even keel, and after a dithering pause, fell over with a crash in the other direction. Under a cloudless sky this silly performance went on and on. True, the sea was roughish, a dark, tumbling mass flecked with white—but the boat was moving about alarmingly. Ever since she had begun rolling in a flat calm the day before, rumours had flown about that she had been refused insurance at Lloyd's; that her superstructures had been built illegally high; that her bows had been shortened to save money, and several other comforting items. Be that as it may, the result was that the plan for a few of the Tell el Amarna staff to get to know each other and to talk over the coming season on the boat between Venice and Alexandria, had gone awry. The three members of the staff were distributed horizontally in various parts of the ship's interior, and were taking no interest in each other or the coming season.

Venice—now two days to the north-west of us—had not been a great success either as a rallying-point. There I had met the two architects of the expedition, and we had first eyed each other cautiously over large plates of spaghetti in a waterside hostelry. They were both fair and blue-eyed, and somehow faintly antagonistic to each other, which struck me as odd, because I knew that they had scarcely met before leaving London. Over a bottle of Chianti, it emerged that Hilary, who looked the younger, was twenty-eight, Ralph was twenty-three; and as in the polite pause that followed I seemed to see a large query mark, in the manner of the comic strip, hovering over either head, I obliged with the information that I was twenty-seven.

"Of course I don't know about the others," said Hilary, "but so far that makes me the oldest." His child-like pleasure at this idea made me wonder if Ralph also had the feeling that we were all sitting round a miniature green-painted table, about to make things out of plasticine. He grinned at me, and I knew that he had.

"What about the Director?" I asked. "Surely——?"

"John?" said Hilary. "I believe he's just twenty-six."

I was startled. We did seem very young as a group to be responsible for a complete excavation. I thought of the few occasions when I had seen the new Director in London. Tow-headed, brooding, rather formidable, but a reassuring picture. He certainly had looked more than his years.

"Personally," Hilary went on, "I don't much like the idea of working for a man two years my junior."

"What's his age got to do with it?" Ralph said grumpily. "And didn't you know he's also the Curator at Knossos? Anyway he knows the site at Amarna, which is more than most of the rest of us."

"One season—as a Field Assistant."

"Perhaps he was a very good Field Assistant," I said mildly. "Anyway we shouldn't have dug at all this winter if the committee hadn't agreed that he was the man for it—I know that. And they should know."

We finished lunch without further argument, while the golden reflections from the water below the open window rippled unceasingly across the low white ceiling, and the Chianti whispered to us its comfortable story of southern sunshine.

That was two days ago, and we had hardly met since. By the

second day, I was very tired of my cabin and its other occupants. One was a nun who kept the door locked all the time, presumably as a symbolic protest against the wicked world, which infuriated me every time I wanted to get in and—as the lock was very stiff—terrified me every time I wanted to get out. The other was a little hospital nurse who had been very ill, and had been sent off for a convalescent sea holiday. Every time the ship rolled she fell out of her bunk, usually on to her trunk as it slithered down the frightening slope of the deck, "and if this is a pleasure-cruise," she would remark, climbing grimly back again, "Lord, give me a wet Sunday in the Mile End, any day!"

I took a rug and some books and found the way up to the lifeboat deck. No one was about, and although it seemed dizzily high above the water, the exhilaration of being in the sun and wind took away the last vestige of queasiness. The sky was softly, brilliantly blue, the tumbling sea inky-dark, except astern where a broad smooth road of emerald, creaming and frothing, marked our passing.

I found a long wooden chair and wedged it as much out of the wind as possible between the curve of a lifeboat and the white rail. The boat was still rolling strongly, but I was getting used to it, and anyway we were still the right way up, so that there now seemed a reasonable chance of gaining the harbour at Alex. There was a confusion of good sounds and smells. The endless smash and hiss of the great bow waves, flung back on to the choppy surface; the creak of all the straining woodwork as the huge ship laboured on; the strong scent of fresh paint and of seasoned wood, warm in the sun; above all the salt in the sparkling air. The white rail climbed and dropped, the far horizon sank and lifted, the quivering halliards and hawsers hummed a high shrill note in the wind. All the stress of the journey and the tiring preparations for it were forgotten, swept away like the feather of dark smoke flicking away from the giant funnel above me. For a little I hung blissfully between two worlds, lost in the blank beauty of a perfect moment.

Then I remembered the task that I had set myself for these few days—till now neglected—and drew from a coat pocket a small green book. A manual of spoken Arabic. I had been told that no one at Tell el Amarna beyond the staff would know any English, so that it was essential to learn at least enough Arabic to make oneself understood. I hoped that it wouldn't stop at that, and that eventually not only would They understand Me, but that I would understand Them, which sounded a lot more interesting. However, this might be over-ambitious; and after some time with my manual, I was fairly certain that it was. For one thing, most of the words seemed to be peppered with apostrophes, and also had a startling way of ending in 'q'—and a 'q' deprived of the customary 'u' alongside has such an unfinished look; like a face without eyebrows. As regards the apostrophes, I learned from a sober little footnote on page 1 that they did indeed represent a sound, and had to be pronounced, but—and this seemed a bit discouraging—no one who was not an Arab born could hope to produce it correctly. As it was too late now to do anything about that, I supposed that I should never master this point. I went on to the vocabulary, and marked with a pencil all the nouns I could see that might be most usefully learned first. 'Bread, water, fire, house, money' —that seemed a good basic bunch to begin with. I looked carefully away from anything that might not come in handy, but try as I would, I kept noticing that the word for 'violet' was 'banafsiga'; and as I have a talent, amounting to genius, for remembering useless details at the expense of useful ones, that word stuck. I may say that I never once saw a violet in Egypt; never once needed urgently to say 'banafsiga'; but whereas the words for bread, water, fire, house and money had to be hammered into my head by concentrated effort and kept there

27

by constant practice, 'banafsiga' perched, fragrantly and effortlessly in my brain from the start.

How about the verbs? I found one spread out in full, chosen because it was regular and typical, the 'amo', apparently, of Arabic. It was spelled *Laff*, and, rather unfortunately in the circumstances, meant 'to roll'. I spent most of the afternoon on that verb; and although by the time I got to Tell el Amarna, I still could neither walk nor run in Arabic, I could have rolled from one end of the dig to the other in any mood or tense you cared to mention.

What did I know about the dig itself by this time? A good deal more than I had known a few months ago, but even so it was still only a hazy outline. I shut the manual, and leaned back to rest, eyes closed, face full in the hot sun. It was a good moment to try and summarize the rather jumbled information that I had collected over the past few months. I had spent a good deal of spare time reading about it and looking at photographs, and now knew just enough of the history of Egypt to be able to visualize a background against which I could set the site and its history. Today, many people with no special knowledge of Egyptology have a good general idea of Tell el Amarna and its significant features, because so much has been written about it in a semi-popular way, and also because the starting-point of historical education in England has been travelling further and further back so illuminatingly in recent times. It's a long time, of course, since English schoolchildren learned to look undaunted into the blue distance stretching behind the once uncompromising barrier of 1066 and all that; and, as the view became clearer, to take first Rome, and then Greece, in their infant stride. But today they know that the roots run even further, tapering away, thin but still strong, to Egypt and Babylonia and beyond.

But even so, there must be many people who, even if they can roughly visualize the vast uneasy undulating plain of

Egyptian history, broken by its foothills of transient power, its valleys of anarchy, its three tremendous peaks of achievement which were the Old Kingdom, the Middle, and the New, have never looked in detail at any one particular point in that landscape, and may never have heard of Tell el Amarna, the site of Akhenaten's City. Of these I'd been one, long after school days were over; so here I paused, swinging between heaven and earth, feeling already a glow of sunburn spreading over face and hands, while I tried to marshal what facts I could remember.

As I know that I am not unique in visualizing history in a mental picture, with upland and valley, light and shade and change of direction, it is perhaps simple to describe the historical place of Akhenaten's strange and brief adventure as lying just this side of, and a little below, the peak of the New Kingdom. The struggle of others to achieve and hold a vast Empire, stretching from Nubia to Syria, is behind him; Akhenaten stands on the last great slope. The slope does not dive down from there unbroken to obscurity; ahead, and yet below, are still the great uplands of the Dynasty of the Ramses, before the final levelling. But high though his position is, it is none of his making: the achievement was that of his near ancestors, for the light in which he stands bathed for ever is that of the westering sun.

More prosaically, the New Kingdom stretched roughly from a little before 1500 B.C. to a little before 1000 B.C., and Akhenaten himself ruled from about 1370 for seventeen years. The New Kingdom had come to its height by the time his father, Amenhotep III, came to the throne.

Already decay had set in. Trouble was on every frontier; and the heir to this splendid headache was a young man who cared nothing for the dust and heat of battle or the power that great possessions bring. The following bare facts are admittedly a colossal over-simplification of an astonishing event in history. For it is the story of one of the earliest voices crying in the wilderness that the things of this world, that most men think worth fighting for, are bitter in their reward and hollow.

Briefly, he discarded the ancient many-sided gods of his fathers, Amun its chief god, and became absorbed in the idea of a single god, creator and sustainer of all things. This god was personified by the disk of the sun, the Aten, and to the sun Akhenaten addressed all his worship. From the name Amenhotep, the fourth Amenhotep of his line, he turned away, and took that of Akhenaten, 'it is well with the Aten'. The rift and strife in the great capital of Thebes between priests and Pharaoh became intolerable; there was trouble at home, trouble on the frontiers, trouble everywhere. Some have called Akhenaten a weak escapist; some see him as a deeply spiritual man of great moral courage; some as a shrewd politician making this break with the priests through no spiritual conviction, but as a means of crushing their power which was threatening that of Pharaoh. But the fact emerges from these differences of opinion, which if they bring us no nearer to the truth about the character of the Pharaoh, at least are highly revealing in themselves as assessments of the critics, that the decision taken by that long dead man can still arouse deep feelings in those who know his story, more than three thousand years after his death.

In the sixth year of his reign Akhenaten and his wife Nefertiti—that beautiful lady whose very name means 'the beautiful lady comes'—their children, their friends and any who cared to follow them to an unknown life, sailed northwards from angry Thebes to inhabit a new-built city where the new religion might flourish unchecked. Akhenaten had declared that this city must be built on virgin soil, standing on ground never before dedicated to another god.

A few years earlier, soon after his accession, he had discovered what he wanted, two hundred miles north of Thebes. On the east bank of the Nile, high back-sloping cliffs march close with the windings of the river for many miles. But here they break away, sweeping back in a deep curve to rejoin the river at a point about seven miles to the north. It is like a strung bow, the greatest width of the land enclosed being about three miles across. Here, sheltered in the embrace of the cliffs, close to the lifegiving river, the City of Akhenaten rose up at Pharaoh's command, fresh, glittering, dedicated; quays and harbours, temples and palaces, gardens and groves. Here, drifting down from Thebes, the little fleet dropped anchor; and life began in palaces and houses where the paint and plaster were scarcely dry, where hammer and chisel still rang and rasped with feverish activity.

The city which he called Akhetaten (Horizon of the Disk)— lasted less than twenty-five years. Akhenaten lived there for eleven years, and after his death was succeeded by his young half-brother, a child of ten called Tutankhaten.

The priests of Amun were not slow to move. A few years more and the young Pharaoh had agreed to change his name, significantly, to Tutankhamun, and had returned amid great rejoicing to the ancient capital and religion of his fathers. For a little while, life in Akhenaten's city flickered on—perhaps those who stayed behind thought that its glory would come again. But none returned from Thebes. Slowly the city crumbled; the sand blew in and over the deserted ruins; and at last there was nothing left but a great waste of gently undulating sand dunes, asleep in the silence and the sun.

From that time, somewhere in the middle of the fourteenth century B.C., until the middle of the nineteenth century A.D., the City of Akhenaten was unknown and unguessed. Where once the quays and harbours glittered white along the river front, a strip of cultivation grew, and two or three mud villages came into being, shaded by thick palm groves. Behind lay the sand-dunes baking in the sun, hidden from the river by the palms, unheeded by the waterside villagers.

One day in the 1880's a village woman wandered a little

way inland from the cultivation to dig among the dunes for rubble manure. She dug up many little hard clay objects; and noticing marks scratched in the clay, took them across the river; for by that date it would be a subnormal Egyptian, however humble, who did not spot the possibility of an 'antika', and a consequent odd coin or so wrung from a grumbling dealer. What she received is unknown, but it was most certainly inadequate reward; for after being offered to one museum after another, and rejected and taken round and about, suffering breakage and even loss, the crumbling collection of tablets was at last recognized as actual letters written to the then shadowy figure known as the heretic Pharaoh Akhenaten, and therefore, of first-class importance, not for their contents alone. They were the correspondence to his Foreign Office. Some of them came from loyal vassal kings, vainly struggling to hold the northern fringe of the Empire, imploring aid (which never came) from Pharaoh against the enemies who beset them all about.

But where had these tablets been found, asked the translators, as the significance of the letters began to emerge? The site was traced; after more than three thousand years a city that had once been the short-lived capital of a great Empire was discovered. For many years after, until the mid-thirties, excavators from different countries held concessions there in turn, digging and publishing, gradually revealing not only a clear picture of a way of life which broke clean away from the old traditions of Egyptian religion and of art, but even something of the personality of its strange author.

Here we were, then, the latest recruits to this strange business of archaeology, this living backwards in order to accelerate, by however little, the forward surge of present knowledge.

We were the heirs to a site which was by now famous through the labours of many others, among them Petrie in 1891; and it was here during the period when a German expedition held the concession before the 1914–18 War, that the world-famous head of Nefertiti was found in a sculptor's workshop. Yet much of the city still lay below its obliterating sand —and until the last house was planned, the last rubbish heap sorted, there was no saying what exquisite things might not be lying beneath, to be rescued in the course of clearing the buildings.

Suddenly I caught again the intensity of the moment when I had first seen the little glazed tile with its lotus flower design. I still felt shy of the unknown staff—still felt sad at leaving my clay girl; but surging up through all that and beginning to swamp it completely was an undeniable exhilaration, as every plunge of that wicked old ship meant a few less yards to go before I looked with my own eyes on all that was left of Akhenaten's city.

Chapter Four

THE three of us were met at the station at Cairo by the philologist of the expedition, the only member besides the Director who was an archaeologist by profession and had done field work before. His first charge was of course all the inscriptional material that would be found during the season. But like everyone else on the staff, he was to become involved in all the other problems which cropped up; partly because the staff was not really big enough to cope with all the work, but mostly because on a dig there really are no watertight compartments; every discovery in each department has its bearing on all the others.

Tommy was, like us, in the twenties. He was a tall, bony, fresh-faced young man, with a streamlined profile which seemed to be for ever plunging, hawk-like, after an elusive inscription—but with the bland and humorous eyes of a budding professor behind gold-rimmed glasses. He told us that he had reached Cairo a week before, and had been working at the Museum, and that John and Mrs. John had only just arrived.

"They're at the Continental," he said, " and hope we'll all go round there for dinner. I've got you all rooms at the Victoria where I am. Much cheaper and quite pleasant—and anyway we're only here for three days."

The four-hour train journey from Alexandria had done nothing to restore my land legs. The rolling of the ship had disturbed my balancing apparatus to such an extent that it took days to right itself, and my chief recollection of Cairo is of a very hot city with pavements that rocked from side to side.

We trailed round together to the Continental after sunset, just as the evening chill crept down the wide streets, and the

35

immense palms shivered in the lamplight. Here, where the shops displayed all the dazzling sophistication of Europe, and glittering cars moved past towards Shepheard's and the Opera House, Tell el Amarna seemed a thousand miles away, rather than a little over two hundred. We were welcomed by Mrs. John, who told us that although they had only arrived that morning, John had already put through a good deal of business about the concession of the dig, and had seen the Museum officials. She was small and blue-eyed and cheerful, and I think we both felt relieved that there was another woman on the dig.

John arrived; and we moved in to dinner. Under cover of the general conversation, I had a chance to look at him carefully for the first time. He was on the tall side, but with a breadth of shoulder that seemed a little to diminish the impression. Otherwise he had the slim build and—I had already seen—the springing step of the trained athlete; and indeed triumphs of high-jumping at Cambridge lay only a few years behind him. Yet already there was a hint of the increasing weight which maturity so often brings to the athlete. And so it was, I had a feeling, with his mind; here, at this first gathering, was only to be seen an easy, light-hearted manner, as he told us of an encounter of the afternoon which had amused him—at the moment there seemed to be no connection here with the absorbed and withdrawn figure I had encountered in London; but yet, as one watched, one became aware of the same feeling of controlled and concentrated power, even while he laughed.

If he felt any justifiable qualms that evening as he surveyed his raw and scarce-known colleagues, he didn't show it: he and his wife alone knew the site and that for one winter's work only. In his first year as Director the work that he planned to do was to be helped or hindered by four young strangers, three without any experience of excavation; besides that, he had to organize and control the native labourers, upwards of a hundred of them.

Towards the end of dinner, plans for the next day were discussed, and a very subtle new note invaded the now easy atmosphere. Up till then we had felt ourselves no more than guests at his table—a pleasant but not quite authentic relationship. We were in a mood to welcome some direction, to make the reality of the season's work come a little nearer. Then John said, "I thought you all might like to come to the Museum tomorrow morning—and then I thought we might go out to the Pyramids in the afternoon. Then that will leave a clear day for final shopping before we go south." Of course we all were keen to go to the Museum and the Pyramids, and of course the "I thought you might like . . ." suggested that anyone was perfectly free to stay behind who wasn't. But all the same—there was a certain something behind that mild invitation which was unmistakable; we were expected to fall in with a thought-out programme. We were companions, but no longer merely guests—we were already like junior officers, crowded round a map on a table, listening to a plan; the campaign was beginning.

I can remember wonderfully little of that first visit to the Cairo Museum and its magnificent collections, largely because my energies were still bent on navigating the heaving ground. One of the English officials drove us there, a fierce little man with a smouldering eye and a heart of gold, grey hair crowned by the Egyptian tarbush, a dark red fez, badge of officialdom. As we climbed out of his car in the forecourt of the Museum, his attaché-case burst open and the contents were whipped away all over the place in a sudden strong breeze. We rushed about retrieving his property, my contribution amounting to several corrected galley-proofs of a learned book peppered with hieroglyphs, and a printed song entitled, "'Ow I 'ates women."

We spent most of our time, naturally, looking at the finds from Tell el Amarna itself, greeting like old friends the originals never before seen and yet completely familiar through their photographs in London. Here was the exquisite little sandstone head of one of Akhenaten's six daughters, the sweet full mouth, and the long, strange-shaped head. Here the neck-lace whose description I had deciphered one gloomy February morning. The great ornament, six rows deep, lay here shining softly, blue of grape and cornflower, red of date fruit, and yellow and white of flower petals.

When we arrived at Gizeh in the afternoon, I discovered that as well as observing them from a safe distance, the plan included a trip into the interior of one of the Pyramids—the Great Pyramid to be exact. As I have, in common with many people, a horror of confined spaces, this expedition was something of a nightmare. But there was nothing for it—I could not hang back at the outset of my adventures in Egypt. If the others were all going in, I must go too. So I clenched my teeth, told myself that it was unlikely that the Great Pyramid would choose that particular Tuesday afternoon to disintegrate, and plunged after the others into the small, rough aperture on the north side of the vast pile. In my ignorance I had somehow expected the tomb chambers to be at ground level, but the passage at once turned upwards and a long incline could just be made out, dimly lit by a few wide-apart electric bulbs. The passage roof was very high. Underfoot, wooden slats, nailed across the ramp, gave useful foothold. A guide went ahead, and we pressed after him, while an occasional vast bat swept in the gloom past our shrinking heads. At the top of the slope we came to the lofty King's Chamber, and at the sight of the great empty tomb, stood silently in the presence of that relic of tremendous majesty. In silence we left the chamber; climbed down the ramp again a little way, to a point where another passage broke away from it. This passage was horizontal, and so low that no one could stand upright in it. It ran immediately below the higher ramp we had climbed and opened into another smaller room. It was very strange to stand in that chamber, knowing that one was somewhere high up in the very core of that vast pyramid. Masonry not only pressing in on us on every side and from above, but below as well. At last we began the downward climb, and as a glimmer of sunlight began to filter up the walls below, the feeling of being a slightly hysterical currant in an outsize bun began to leave me. Two days later we left Cairo.

It was evening when our train drew in at the station of Mallawi. All the afternoon it had ambled down the western bank of the Nile, sometimes close to the water's edge, sometimes moving through endless fields of maize and cotton. The sun blazed down on the carriage roof. We kept the windows shut most of the time in a vain attempt to keep out the white clouds of dust. But the taste of dust was in our throats. On the far side of the river, the high limestone cliffs kept us company, sometimes far away, sometimes just beyond the river. At every wayside station groups of cheerful peasants crowded the platforms, apparently just for the fun of seeing the train go by. They looked very jolly, and very different from their city brothers. Some of them had oranges to sell, and we bought them gladly as we grew more and more thirsty.

On the platform at Mallawi a fine, tall Egyptian beautifully dressed, with a purple embroidered over-cloak above a spotless white tunic, and a purple silk head-dress, came forward and made his salaams to John and Hilda. He touched first his forehead and then his breast with his fingers and then took their outstretched hands. This was Hussein Abu Bakr, trusted

servant of the Society, who had been instructed to open up the Expedition House and have all in readiness. Behind him stood his brother Abd el Latif, cook to the establishment, and their nephew, a boy who was always known as Young Abu Bakr, who was being trained as a houseboy by Uncle Hussein. A little behind these stood three or four beaming locals, the small but significant gap between the two parties showing clearly that the Abu Bakr family, who came from Abydos far up the Nile, and owned a big rambling house there, were a cut above the village folk of Tell el Amarna.

John and Hilda made introductions all round in enviably fluent Arabic. Hussein explained that he had hired two cars to take us and the luggage to the river bank, here about half a mile away. John gave in to the practical arrangement, although he hated driving when it was possible to walk, and we all managed to get into the leading car, while the Abu Bakr family, entirely submerged, except for three large grins, by the pile of suitcases, followed in the other. The locals loped cheerfully behind in the dust. We were hot, dusty and tired, and the short car trip brought us nearly to breaking point. It was completely terrifying. Soon after the road left the station, it ran on to the top of a kind of high dyke which wound unfenced between the cultivated fields which lay anything from ten to twenty feet below. At the time of the annual Nile flood, these fields would with luck be well under water, renewed by the rich deposit of mud which is Egypt's life-blood. The high dykes which ran criss-cross all over the cultivation would then be the only means of moving about dry-footed. Some of the time the width of the dyke top was comfortingly greater than that of the car—but more often there didn't seem anything to choose between them. The driver liked seeing how fast he could go round the bends without falling off. Sometimes a bit of the dyke had collapsed, leaving a hollow scoop on one side over which the wheels bounced. Sometimes a camel had to be driven round. It was a wonderful moment when at last the track sloped down between two fields and we saw the water of the Nile lapping at our feet.

The river was very wide here and this evening very calm. Behind us the sun was near the horizon. Far away across the water, a long line of palms stood motionless, their images clear in the river. Above them the cliffs soared upward, golden-flushed.

Moored to a rickety landing-stage close to where we stood, was a strange-looking craft. It had served the expeditions at Tell el Amarna for many a long year. It was about twenty feet in length, and seemed to be made up of a conglomeration of many odd pieces of different kinds and lengths of wood, representing so many repairs that there was hardly any of the original boat left. The mast was stepped, with a very bulky sail furled round it, like an untidily rolled umbrella. We climbed in dubiously and in a miraculously short time all the suitcases were stowed away somewhere in the tub-like depths. We were at a point still about a mile north of the site, and as we were moving against the current, the first stage of the river passage was done by a tow-rope. At a signal from Hussein the villagers, scarcely sweating or short of breath after their trot from the station, seized the long rope attached to the bows, and moved off in single file along a well-worn track which ran up and down the bank. The old felucca followed sedately with its closely packed cargo of passengers and suitcases. The water level seemed uncomfortably near the gunwales.

Sometimes the men towing were walking along the water's edge with the bank rising above their heads. Sometimes the path led them steeply up till they marched black against the blazing sunset, and the drops of water dancing off the tow-rope flashed like jewels. Hussein sat at the tiller carefully holding the bows of the craft off the bank.

The direction turned a little to the right and a new stretch of the river came into view. Away on the eastern bank the golden cliffs came to a headland that sloped down nearly to the water's edge. The line of palm trees at its foot went on alone along the river bank beyond. John pointed. " That is the northern limit of the site." We stared across the golden water as the boat slowly drew level with the majestic outpost of the City. "And there," he went on, pointing south to where, far away in the evening haze, dim and grey and low in the distance, another headland dipped towards the water, "can you see it? That is the southern headland. Akhenaten rounded that cliff when he first came here from the south."

We were just above the northern headland now. The men on the tow-rope stopped and drew the boat towards them. Carefully they coiled in the rope, and two of them stepped aboard, and fitted themselves somehow on to the middle thwart, and thrust out two rough oars. The others squatted down on the bank to wait patiently for a later trip across. The felucca now headed straight across the river for a tiny landing-stage just south of the headland.

It was very peaceful and cool, and utterly beautiful. No one wanted to talk. The sun went down. Now we could see a few white-clad figures moving among the trees as we drew near. Blue smoke trailed up here and there above the feathery palms. The felucca grated gently against the landing-stage, and Hussein and the two oarsmen gave steadying hands as we climbed to the bank. A narrow path sloped up to the trees, and along it we went in single file till it wound through the dark clearing under the palms. Men, women and children were waiting here to watch the unusual procession, full of smiles and half-military salutes and shy greetings. The path soon wound to the fringe of the trees on the landward side. We came into the evening light again. Before us lay a billowing stretch of brown sand-dunes. And riding the billows like a long, low ship just ahead of us was the house which would be our home. Brown as the sand where it rested, rambling, friendly-looking; and someone was walking towards us to light the darkening path with a lantern.

Above the house the cliffs, turning away now from the river, seemed to be growing bright again; and as we moved towards the house, they slowly flushed to purple, rose and gold in the strange afterglow of the sunset.

Chapter Five

I LIKE to think I've lived in a house more than three thousand years old. For our Expedition House was simply a restored house of Akhenaten's time. To get an idea of the look of the site and the position of the house in it, imagine again the strung bow lying along the Nile. Akhenaten had built a waterside city, so that nearly all the remains lie straggling along—and beneath—the cultivation. The great curve of the bow—the limestone cliffs—sweeps round the site from north to south, the headlands coming quite near to the Nile, but leaving plenty of space at their foot for the palms and dusty camel track to continue along the river. Behind the city lies a vast, almost semi-circular sandy plain, washing up to the cliffs, gently rolling where no ancient buildings lie beneath, but a choppy brown sea where crumbling walls lie like submerged rocks.

We had penetrated the 'bow' almost at the northern tip, for the house lay fairly near the corner where string and bow almost met, tucked between cliffs and trees. As we came out from beneath the darkening trees into the still warmly-glowing desert, and saw the house quite near with its welcome of lamp-light, I felt an answering glow of happiness inside me. After the strange, hot, tiring journey, passing through the mono-tonous flat land of the western side for hour after hour, there was a quite unexpected effect of snug homeliness about the whole setting. At the entrance we paused while stacks of suit-cases were sorted out. Looking back through the palms I could just see the river faintly shining. North and eastwards the friendly cliffs—still sun-warmed—threw a protecting arm round the house. Only to the south lay the great open sweep of the sandy plain and the main ruins of the city. John was looking that way, as we went in.

The house was nearly square, and had rooms round three sides of a small courtyard. The fourth side—the one nearest the river—was now a low wall about two feet high with a gap in the middle. This led into what had once been the West Loggia, a big room running the length of the west side of the house, now of course open to the sky. You crossed it and went through a gap (an original doorway) in its inner wall, into the central courtyard. The first thing you noticed in the courtyard were four beautifully cut, stone circular bases, about four feet in diameter and six inches high, fixed in the beaten earth floor. These were column bases, for our small courtyard had once been the main Central Room of the house, with a roof supported by four tall, wooden columns painted red, a roof that soared above the surrounding rooms, so that its high windows could give clerestory lighting. You could still see the marks of red paint on the bases, round the carefully incised cross in the centre, which the mason had cut to ensure the exact centring of the pillar. The original walls of the house when excavated some years before were still standing as high as five or six feet in places, and were in such good condition that all that was needed was to build on to them a bit and then re-roof the rooms. All the rooms round the Central Room—now the courtyard—were built up on the original foundations and kept the plan of the ancient builder, with wooden roof supports—no graceful pillars now unfortunately—resting once again on the stone bases. On the south-west corner was a fairly large room always occupied now by the Director of the moment, and next it, on the south end of the Loggia, and connected with the Director's room, was his office, a large, bare sandy room, mostly furnished with rough shelves, a table under each of the two windows, which looked out, one into the loggia, the other towards the dig.

The Director's room jutted a little beyond the outer wall of the house, and was in fact the original porch. There were traces of two or three steps leading up to it against the outside of the western wall. The old Egyptian family and their visitors must have used these steps to reach the porch, then turned left into our office (probably then a sort of cloakroom) then left again through the door into the southern end of the long West Loggia, and so half right into the Central Room. Our own method of walking straight across the remains of the West Loggia through gaps in the middle of its two long sides was certainly a lot quicker, if not so interesting.

Next to the office was a long slip of a room used by the architects. The rest of the south side was taken up by the main living-room. It was large and dark and cool, with mats over the earthen floor, two big column bases in the centre, over which the new members of the staff fell continuously for the first week, a long table for meals and for work, a wildly uncomfortable native sofa bristling with sharp bits of bamboo at the most unexpected moments, one or two rather tentative wicker chairs and wooden stools, and a bookshelf. High up in the wall on the courtyard side were two small square windows. No windows on the south side, but two doors, each leading to a small room with a window looking out towards the dig. The one on the right was the antiquity room and was lined with wooden shelves from floor to ceiling on either side. These shelves were like a silent challenge. Quite empty now; but through the season they would fill up, very gradually, day by day; much of what we found would be, I knew, repetitions of well-known common objects, and yet there was always the chance, just the chance, of something finding its way there, the like of which had never been seen before, something which would turn the little dark mud-brick room into a treasure-house. . . .

The other small room had a low coffee table, two more

groggy wicker chairs, and one dead lizard. It had an air about it as if someone a long time ago—probably an excavator's wife —had made the mistake of thinking that there would be time to relax at Amarna. It was a sort of pathetic attempt at a tiny drawing-room. Nobody ever used it, and eventually I commandeered it for an extra place to clean antiquities in. Judging from the evidence from other excavated houses, built on very much the same plan, our living-room and these two little rooms leading off it were probably a vestibule with two guest rooms beyond it.

On the east side of the courtyard were three more bedrooms and a photographic dark-room full of nameless horrors and worse smells.

On the north side store-rooms. And on the extreme north-west corner, leading out of the north side of the ancient West Loggia, the kitchen.

My own room opened off the courtyard on the east side. It was long and narrow, with just enough room for a camp-bed, mosquito net, primitive wash-stand and camp-chair. There was a tiny window in the very thick eastern wall, looking out towards the receding cliffs. On this side the house was buried in sand-dunes up to window level, so that the bottom of the window was at ground-level if you were looking at it from outside. It was covered with strong fine netting, which I resented until a day when Hussein showed me the clear track of a big snake in the sand close up against the netting. There was a small oil-lamp with a reflector hanging on a nail on the brown mud-plaster wall, and a few hooks behind the door. I had to keep all my clothes in my suitcases. It was rough, spotlessly clean and adorable.

As soon as we had found our way to our rooms that first evening, Young Abu Bakr appeared at my door with a can of boiling water, and set it carefully and silently in the basin. Like his uncles he wore an ankle-length one-piece of dazzling white, and a white linen pork-pie on the back of his head. I said "Khattar kherak" nervously—my little green book having assured me that that was right for 'Thank you'. At this his solemn little face broke into a melon-slice smile, and he went off into a rattle of musketry which was either a speech of welcome or compliments on the astonishing grasp I had of his native tongue. Luckily he bowed himself out at the same time, so for the moment was spared utter disillusion.

One by one we trailed into the living-room, and our first meal together at Amarna began. We were all pretty tired. John at one end of the table, Hilda at the other. Ralph and Hilary against the wall on one side, Tommy and I negotiating the column bases on the other. A huge oil-lamp hung from a beam above the table. The door to the courtyard was wide open in the warm evening air. Now and then a locust, like a hinged monkey nut, slammed into the room, blundered about a bit and then hurtled out again.

A swish of linen robes came across the courtyard, and here was Hussein with a vast soup tureen, followed by Abu Bakr, like an acolyte, reverently bowed over a bowl of croutons

BATHTIME

instead of incense. Abd el Latif's special lentil soup, followed by Abd el Latif's special spinach pie (which had eggs and cheese in it), followed by freshly picked tangerines and bananas, and very sweet red-hot coffee —it sounds simple, but still ranks very high in my list of memorable meals.

After the table had been cleared, we sat and talked for a little while. I think John was exhilarated but exhausted. He had put through all the preliminary negotiations and had got us here, and was now on the threshold of a big responsibility. He must have wondered again that evening, as he looked at us, how we were going to make out. Were we going to understand his feeling for the place, and go all out to help make a success of this, his first season as Director, or would any of us, perhaps all of us, let him down? I don't know what he was thinking. All he said, as we broke up for the night and came out again into the courtyard, was: "We'll take on the men in the morning. In the afternoon we'll go down to the site and have a look round, and see how much sand has drifted in in the summer. Hussein says the Guftis will be here in the course of the day. We can finish unpacking the equipment and getting straight in the evening. Then we'll begin digging the day after to-morrow. Good night." Hilda added that we mustn't mind the jackals if we heard any. They lived in the high desert at the top of the cliffs, and sometimes came down at night to drink. Also to spray the inside of our mosquito nets with the sprays that were in every room. Also to shake our garments in the morning just in case of an enterprising scorpion looking for warmth. That made me feel a little thoughtful. But my little bare room looked very warm and safe in the soft light of the oil-lamp. At the door I looked back. I could see right across the courtyard and over the low walls of the West Loggia to the river. The courtyard was still in deep shadow, but a full moon, just clear of the cliffs behind me, was flooding the ground beyond. The quiet palm groves along the river were all silver and grey—the river gleamed between the tree trunks—and to the north the headland shone white.

At last I was in bed and took the flyspray with me and bedewed the inside of the net till I was almost buzzing like a dying mosquito myself. Then I carefully tucked the ends of the net into the mattress all round, making a little tent. It was fuggy but felt very safe. Then I realized that the lamp was still alight,

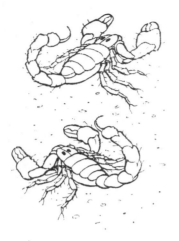

so I undid it all again. Then I didn't like the idea of treading on a scorpion in the dark. So I unhooked the lamp and stood it by the bed and got into my cocoon again, leaving just enough gap to put an arm out to reach the lamp. I turned it out. There was already utter silence outside, so complete that I noticed the faint singing in my ears from the day's fatigue.

A blue spear of moonlight slanted down the wall. There was a faint scrabble in a corner. Did scorpions scrabble? I didn't know, but hoped there were gentle things like mice in Egypt. What on earth were Guftis? "The Guftis will be here in the course of the day." I ought to know. They might be packing-cases, or camels, or inspectors from the Department of Antiquities. I was very sleepy. But suddenly I was wide awake again. Far away, a thin high wail shivered the silence. Then another wail began, and another—and I seemed to see a distraught cloud of wraiths drifting about the ruins all around us, lamenting for their lost lives and ancient homes. Then somewhere a dog barked furiously, and the wailing died away. Quietness washed over everything again. And with it came Hilda's: "Don't mind the jackals if you hear them." Jackals. Any explanation was a comfort at that moment, and I felt better. I grew sleepy again. What a day. Scorpions. Jackals. Guftis. The Guftis are coming, hurrah, hurrah. I began to watch Young Abu Bakr climbing up the Great Pyramid with a can of hot water. But I don't know if he ever got to the top.

Chapter Six

I WOKE up feeling certain it was Sunday. When you are accustomed to waking in Bloomsbury, it is the absence of traffic and footsteps outside in the street which first conveys to you that this is no ordinary working day. But Amarna was like that always. Silence; and the sunshine flooding down into the courtyard as you crossed it in pursuit of coffee and eggs.

It was interesting, that first breakfast, to see how the men had reacted to the question of Correct Wear for Excavations. It isn't too much to say that it gave a clue to personality. John had on a bright pink, open-necked shirt and navy shorts, with a many-coloured belt of twisted leather. Also his hair was standing up thickly, instead of being slicked down on his head. He looked entirely different from his up-to-Amarna self, and much more approachable. I didn't know then how he revelled in medievalism—that when he doodled, as he frequently did when thinking out a dig problem, his doodles were nearly always of knights in armour, or crested helmets, or fine fifteenth-century gallants with wonderful lillypipe hats trailing to the ground. Behind his normal façade of conventional Public School and University man was someone pining for a slashed doublet instead of a neat grey pin-stripe. I think his bright shirts—all his Amarna shirts were pink or green or blue—were something of a gesture. Amarna for him wasn't only a professional excursion into the ancient past. It was also a personal chance to turn his back for a bit on the unromantic aspects of the present.

Tommy, on the other hand, looked exactly like an embryo professor in the field. Very neat and seemly in khaki shirt and shorts. Ralph looked uncomprisingly like any Englishman anywhere in England. A sleeveless black cardigan over a white shirt, and grey flannel bags. He might have been having breakfast in a Chelsea studio or a Cotswold pub. But Hilary was our star turn. He came in to breakfast last, looking as if he had just discovered Livingstone. He was carrying a brand-new topee, which he laid carefully on the bookcase; and wearing a wonderful khaki tunic with a tight belt which he said was called a bush jumper. It had so many pockets, full of so many useful things, that he could hardly stand up; I think it had slots for cartridges as well. There was even a bulge in his hip pocket until John spotted it and told him gently but firmly to remove the contents. "Not on the dig, my lad," he said. "What sort of impression do you think *that* would make? Jackals on the high desert if you *like*."

We discussed last night's jackals. Then Hussein came in and said "Guftis", and I nearly ran outside with my mouth full. John said something which obviously meant: "Tell them to come to the house" for I caught 'taal hinna' which by now I knew meant 'come here'. Up in Palestine and Syria 'hinna' becomes 'honi', so that there you hear 'Taal honi', and even 'Taal ho'; but few people who hear 'Tally Ho!' ringing over the bare English countryside realize that they are listening to an echo of the Crusades, when veterans came home from Palestine and embroidered their speech with phrases which they had learned in foreign parts. Those veterans are surely the spiritual, if not the actual ancestors of all the people one knows who, retired or on leave from the East, talk about 'tiffin' and the 'Memsahib'.

The Guftis turned out to be about twenty men from the small town of Guft, near Luxor, some two hundred miles to the south. Guft is a form of Koptos, and gives its name to the Coptic Christians, whose church was founded, according to legend, by St. Mark himself. In ancient days it was a flourishing trading town, lying at the western end of a caravan route through the barren desert to the sea-coast at Quseir on the Red Sea. Nowadays, its prosperity gone, it has another curious distinction. It is the source from which most of the highly-skilled native diggers are drawn. The reason is that Petrie, digging there as a young man, began to train a small company of the locals to work really skilfully under his direction; and from then on they passed this technique to their sons and grandsons, so that today they still go out to many different digs, and might be said to be the N.C.O.s of field archaeology —drawn from the ranks, but sometimes more knowledgeable in this work than the young European Field Assistant who is gaining his experience. They can rescue the plan of a buried building—however ruined—out of apparent chaos. Also they are each in charge of a group of the local villagers whose main job is just to clear back rubble from the wall which the Gufti himself is delicately tracing.

They stood in a long line beyond the parapet wall, mostly tall men, in dark blue or black robes, carrying tall staves. They wore brilliantly white turbans, wrapped about their heads in lines that were miracles of romantic dignity. Usually one end of the fringed headdress stuck up like a small panache, while the other fell down on the other side of the proud dark face. If they had been fair-skinned it would have been almost like walking back into our own fifteenth century as we came out to greet them.

The Headman was old Umbarak, wrinkled and a little anxious; he had three sons with him, Mohammed, burly and placid, Mahmud, much more delicately built and nervous, and Kassar, a beautiful stripling with wonderful long-lashed eyes and a lock of jet-black hair escaping from his saucy turban. The Guftis all lived together during the season in a small house near our own, which was in fact a restored outhouse belonging to the ancient estate.

This morning the space beyond them was dotted with

groups of men and boys and girls, standing about or squatting on the ground; and more people were coming along the edge of the cultivation, some on donkey back. These had all come from the two main villages in the Amarna cultivation, Et Till, which was quite near us, and Hagg Qandil some miles further south. The word had gone round that the Mudir—the Director —was taking on workmen this morning.

We spent the morning selecting about seventy-five to start with. First the men to do the heavy digging, which they did with a short, wide-bladed hoe called a *tourieh*; and then the basket boys (and girls) who would take the rubble away. They sat in a great semi-circle outside the wall, and the Guftis helped to sort them out, remembering most of them from earlier seasons. No one got a job who was known to have been fired for dishonesty. Everyone taken on was given a printed ticket, which was as vital to him as the English workman's 'cards'. I watched them coming up one by one to get them, like small boys at a prep. school prizegiving. Usually a broad grin, sometimes a military salute, sometimes a dignified word of thanks; and then the slow retreat, with the prize being studied at all angles until it was carefully wrapped up and disposed of somewhere within fold after fold of grimy tunic.

Meanwhile I was making a list of all their names with the rates of pay. In one way it was simple because everybody was called Hussein or Ali or Mohammed or a combination of all three, but for the same reason it was very necessary to get the order right, as I realized when I later found out the way the pay was worked; which was briefly this. The ticket was printed in six divisions, one for each working day of the week. There was also a section marked 'Fines' and another for 'Baksheesh'. At the end of each day on the dig the member of the staff in charge walked along the long line of workmen, clipping a hole with a special star-shaped punch. At one time, the day's work had simply been ticked off with a pencil, until

54

some of the workmen discovered that they could make lovely ticks with a pencil themselves, given a little practice. One of them got a little over-excited at his brilliant get-rich-quick technique, and produced a ticket showing that he had worked eighteen days in one week. Which was the end of him and the beginning of the metal punch. Fines and baksheesh were assessed and written in at the moment when they were earned. Fines were imposed for minor offences of discipline, and baksheesh awarded for some particularly careful piece of digging, or whenever a man found an object as he dug. The main reason for this last was to do away with the temptation for him to try and smuggle a find away and sell it to a dealer. It was difficult to assess rates of baksheesh for some objects, but it had to be very slightly more than he would be likely to get from a dealer. The amount assessed was reduced if the object had been unnecessarily damaged in the course of digging it out. This had the useful effect of making the men as careful as possible when they felt the tourieh touch something solid hidden in the sand.

Baksheesh is the Egyptian's favourite word. As one of us went past a mud house one day, a toddler standing in the doorway removed its finger from its mouth, held out a minute hand, and began: "Bashkeesh, bashkeesh. . . ." There was a scream of horror from Mother somewhere inside. "La! la! Habibi" (No, no,

PAY DAY

Dearie), "BAKSHEESH, *BAK-SHEESH*." Her child would get that word right if she never taught it another thing. She knew her duty as a mother.

Every week the tickets were collected, and part of the evening spent in totting up the totals of time worked, with baksheesh added and fines subtracted. Nearly everybody, therefore, had different sums due on pay-day. So I had to be exceedingly careful. If Hussein Ali Mohammed had been laid off sick for two days, it wouldn't do to mix him up with Ali Mohammed Hussein who had worked full time and found two good amulets; nor would *he* take it kindly if Mohammed Ali Hussein, who had been late to work one day and tapped his neighbour on the nose another, were to get called up on his ticket by mistake.

When we had completed the list of tourieh-men, we took on the children. The boys looked like miniature men, with small head-wraps or round brown felt caps, and white ankle-length shirts. Off-white would be a more accurate description. But the girls were very gay in spite of black head-shawls. They wore long-sleeved cotton frocks of every colour down to their slim brown feet; there was always a glint of cheap bracelets at wrist and ankle and sometimes a gaudy nose-trinket clipped through one nostril. They came up one by one, some shy, a few really beautiful, and the whole lot with the giggles. Everybody was in high spirits, for that matter; even the austere Gufti who was introducing the girls one by one like débutantes at a Drawing room, permitted himself a grave smile when one radiant infant said her name was "Umm' Mohammed, Umm' Mohammed, Umm' Mohammed", Thrice-mother-of-Mohammed; and the listening assembly clearly thought it a scream.

When at last the whole list was complete, the crowd melted away into the cultivation, taking their ten million flies along with them. Abd el Latif rushed out of the kitchen, grumbling

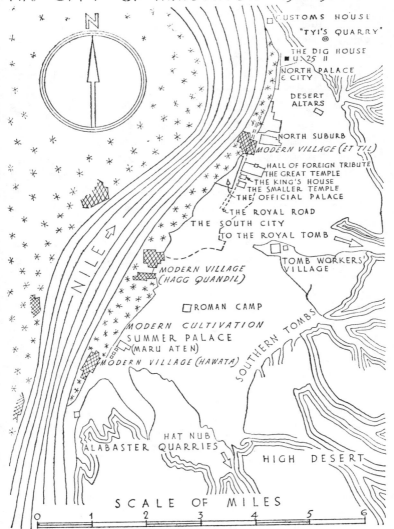

TELL EL AMARNA UPPER EGYPT
THE CITY OF AKHETATEN 1375·1350 B.C.

N

CUSTOMS HOUSE
"TYI'S QUARRY"
THE DIG HOUSE
U 25 11
NORTH PALACE
& CITY
DESERT
ALTARS
NORTH SUBURB
MODERN VILLAGE (ET TIL)
HALL OF FOREIGN TRIBUTE
THE GREAT TEMPLE
THE KING'S HOUSE
THE SMALLER TEMPLE
THE OFFICIAL PALACE
THE ROYAL ROAD
THE SOUTH CITY
TO THE ROYAL TOMB

NILE

MODERN VILLAGE
(HAGG QUANDIL)

TOMB WORKERS'
VILLAGE

ROMAN CAMP

MODERN CULTIVATION
SUMMER PALACE
(MARU ATEN)
MODERN VILLAGE (HAWATA)

SOUTHERN TOMBS

HAT NUB
ALABASTER QUARRIES

HIGH DESERT

SCALE OF MILES

0   1   2   3   4   5   6

horribly, and sped the party on its way with a Flit-gun. He loathed flies, which made him unique among his fellows, and a great comfort, when one thought of his primitive kitchen.

After lunch we all set out for the dig, keeping in the shade which was just beginning to creep out from the cultivation as the sun moved across the river.

It was the first of innumerable walks on the same pattern. Looking back on them I do think that I came by the little I learned of Egyptology, the hard way. Most of it was picked up at the trot in a hot sun. We would start off together, with John discussing some theory or plan as he sprang along over the uneven ground, with everybody round him, listening. Then the striking rate would begin to rise as he talked, and he would draw slowly ahead, Tommy pacing him comfortably, the others either breaking into a gentle lope if the conversation concerned them vitally in their work, or dropping behind if it didn't. Hilda and I usually took our time after the start, and watched the coloured and khaki shirts ahead of us dwindling among the sand-dunes. When we finally pounded up to the dig, John would probably be saying to any survivor something like: "I must say that seems entirely to prove it," or perhaps: "Well, on the evidence, you can't put him higher than seventeen at most." One couldn't very well say at that point, between gasps: "What proves what?" or "*Why* can't you put *who* higher than seventeen, and anyway seventeen *what*?" and expect him to begin all over again. It was all very puzzling and tantalizing at first; and I would reflect sadly that I should find out a lot more about the dig a lot more quickly if only I were five feet ten inches, instead of five feet three.

This first day John was explaining his plan of campaign for the season. The main work was to link up with and continue last season's dig, which had been concentrated on a large isolated group of buildings known as the North Suburb, about a mile south of the Expedition House. Without having yet

58

seen any of it I had a rough idea from looking at plans of the general lay-out of the city.

The Main City had occupied the central part of the 'bow-string' and, of course, had been built first. Down there, about three miles south of our house, I knew that Akhenaten's Palace lay alongside the river. A great main road ran to the east of it and a high bridge, over the road, had once connected it with his private Temple, and also with another Royal House, priests' houses and store-houses. North of this group lay the Great Temple with important houses and official departments nearby. Just east of the private Temple lay the Foreign Office, and it was just here long ago that the famous clay tablets were found—the Foreign Office correspondence which let the first great flood of light in upon the site. A little south of this again lay the main block of private mansions belonging to important officials, and here also lay the sculptor's workshop, where the superb portrait-bust of Nefertiti had been found by the German expedition before the 1914–18 War.

Further south again, two miles or so from the Main City, Akhenaten built a summer palace close to the river, where he could go for rest and refreshment; it had a great shallow lake surrounded by trees and flowers, and here he could drift in light pleasure-craft, picnic beneath the trees, while his six small daughters played about him and Nefertiti, and for a while he could forget his great burden.

All the south and main parts of the city had already been worked over by different groups of archaeologists. Flinders Petrie had done tremendous work there in 1891, a few years after the discovery of the tablets. In Akhenaten's Palace he discovered the painted pavement, one of the finest examples of the startling break with the normal tradition of Egyptian art, which for many people must be the main cause of their fascination for the Amarna period. The pavement covered in all about two hundred and fifty square feet. Here were free, flowing, enchanting scenes of natural life, in soft brilliant colours. Here were small cavorting calves, gambolling through flowering shrubs and reeds to reach the cool water where fish drifted, and heavy lotus flowers swayed in the current. And startled at the solid little calves with their pricking hooves and flicking tails, water-birds clattered up out of the bushes, great wings spread, pink claws drooping and with watchful dewy eyes.

Petrie, with his marvellous practical genius and energy, preserved most of this pavement *in situ*, so that visitors could see it in detail. Luckily there were many unpainted square patches on the floor where the columns had once stood. On these he built low supports to take gang planks and railings, so that a visitor might walk all over the pavement without touching it. He contrived all this himself as he could not trust the local workmen not to drag the planks over the fragile paint.

He covered the whole surface with a thin transparent coating of tapioca, rolling it on with one finger, because he found that even the softest brush tended to drag up the loose frit paint. It was a colossal piece of patient work—and then what happened? About twenty years later, a man who worked the fields which lay between the landing-stage and Palace, became infuriated when tourists, coming to see the pavement, trampled over his crops. Nobody seems to have thought of making a path through the cultivation. So one night he went up to the Palace and hacked the pavement to pieces. All that remains of that unique find today are the drawings and paintings which Petrie made and published, and the small proportion of the original which he managed to raise and transport to the Cairo Museum.

So the slow march of the excavators had come steadily up from the south as the years went by, uncovering a block of houses here, an official building there, moving and pausing, moving and pausing, as the brief seasons came and went.

As we walked south on that hot day we seemed to be moving towards those ghostly pioneers, to the point where their work had ended, where they were waiting for us to take our place in the column, wheel about and then ourselves begin the slow progress northwards once again—digging, clearing, planning, measuring, finding and publishing.

That point was somewhere in the North Suburb, which lay, as I've said, a little north of the Main City, only separated from it by a wide, shallow depression in the ground, a dry *wadi*. Some of it had already been completed in the previous season, with records and plans all in readiness for publication; a little of it was begun but not complete; much of it was entirely drifted over by the sand of more than three thousand years, still untouched, sleeping in the sun. This was the part we reached first as we came down from the house.

We threaded our way over and round and through the confusion of sand heaps; here and there a few sand-coloured bricks broke the rolling surface and stuck up sharp and angular. My own feeling of excitement was rather like that. We were coming to the point at last. The sharp reality of what the expedition was all about was breaking through again, clean and clear, above the jumbled surface of new experiences and odd happenings which in a queer way, although they bore directly on the dig, had somehow a little obscured for me the actual reason for our being there. My head was still full of administrative details—our shopping for equipment in Cairo was only two days back—and for me account books at present bulked much larger than Akhenaten, notebooks than Nefertiti, and the new typewriter had momentarily displaced the New Kingdom. I'd had to concentrate like mad on such details, try to make no mistakes, and forget nothing in the short time available before going off into the blue; with the consequence that I was still in rather a prim secretarial mood when I first came up against the hidden houses of the North Suburb.

We left these behind, and went on a little way to look at part of the excavated suburb. Even to a real Egyptologist it must have looked fairly dilapidated; for the sand of the previous summer had already drifted into the rooms and passages and over the low walls, blurring the clear edges and corners. It looked awful to me, used though I was to the photographs in the London office—and anyway the photographs had at least been taken immediately after the rooms had been perfectly cleared and swept. To a visiting tourist coming between seasons without a proper guide, as some keen tourists did, unless he had a good knowledge of the site's history and the imagination of a seer, the ruins must have been incomprehensible.

Most of the walls stood only a few feet high. But all the doorways and passages and rooms, and the lanes between the houses, were still clear, and we walked in and out of them and listened to John while he explained the more interesting points. It was rather like walking about a new building estate in a way, where the walls are just beginning to rise—the plan is there for all to see, but very little else, and you can see across the walls to where other people, visible from the waist up, are standing about in houses further away.

As well as the great main road which ran the length of the site near the river, there were one or two smaller roads running parallel to it further inland, and these were connected by east–west roads, so that the houses themselves lay in large, roughly rectangular blocks. The owners of the larger, better-planned houses had secured the best positions, for they had built close along the roads, north, south, east and west; the result was that, at first, hollow squares were left in the middle of each block. Gradually these had been filled with poorer houses, the better ones as near to the roads as they could get, and a tangle of hovels and slums in the centre, with tiny lanes and twisting alleyways slipping between the walls of the big estates as the only means of access to the main roads. It was impossible to see this at a glance from a height of five feet three inches above ground level. The whole thing looked like

62

a chaotic tangle of low grey-brown walls, stretching in every direction for hundreds of yards. Short of a helicopter, which would be the ideal way to look at any ancient site—hovering over it at any height you liked, and moving slowly from point to point—I saw that the only thing for me to do was to look at the plans very carefully up at the house, and try gradually to identify the real walls with the drawn.

This sounds more complicated than it was. Actually it was simple. The whole of the site had long ago been surveyed and divided into a system of imaginary squares, lettered and numbered like a district map of London. Each side of the square measured two hundred metres. The lettering ran from west to east, the numbers from north to south. So that to say a house was in square T.36, for instance, considerably narrowed its position on the site. Then each house as it was dug was given its own serial number in addition to its square position, such as T.36.1, and so on. Many of the houses methodically and patiently dug and cleared, and named and numbered, were of little or no interest, and their labels consequently did nothing later on to recall them to mind. But on the other hand, there were some which were so interesting, either because of their splendid planning, or unusual features, or because of the finds which they yielded, that they gave a sort of blaze of glory to their very cut-and-dried labels of identification. It's odd how exciting and familiar the symbol T.36.68 still looks to me even now, years later; simply because of what we found in one of its rooms—to me much more alive and personal a name than Chatsworth or Dunroamin could ever be. It was the same with T.34.1, and T.36.63, when we came to them. But all this lay in the future. Incidentally, our own Expedition House became officially U.25.11, being very slightly to the east, and a good way to the north, of the North Suburb.

The North Suburb lay in the area covered by S, T and U one way, and 32 to 37 the other. My more pernickety readers may be wondering why the western edge of the site so near the river should be adorned with letters so far down in the alphabet. Why not A, B and C? The reason is that the site itself, although almost due north and south in this northern part, develops a strong south-west trend further down, following the river; so that the excavations in the far south of the site strayed westwards into the part of the grid covered by the first letters of the alphabet.

The afternoon was slipping away. We turned back towards the house; everybody looked warm, and already a little flushed with the first day under the clean blessed sun of Amarna. The sun in Cairo had been more of a discomfort than anything else—the light had bounced off hot pavements and glaring walls and had made the already myriad smells much worse. Here there was no unbearable glare—the rays sank into the cool green of the cultivation, into the brown sand, and warmed and purified the ground.

We passed the undug mounds again, and John stopped to show exactly where the digging would begin the next day. Then we trailed on again towards the shady living-room and tea. Ralph was looking happier than I had yet seen him. He shoved his hat back off his warm forehead and began to sing a small Elizabethan song which sounded most peculiar in that setting, but very gay:

> I mean to spend my shoe-sole
> In dancing round the Maypole,
> Turn about, hop and skip,
> And about, in a rout,
> Until very, very weary joints can scarce trip.

The courtyard was full of cases when we got back. The felucca boys had collected them from the station, and had spent the afternoon ferrying them across the Nile. Tinned food, medical supplies, cameras, stationery, cardboard boxes and cotton wool for the finds, the new typewriter—all sorts of things. After tea the cases were opened and we sorted every-thing out. They were mostly in good condition, but one of the cameras, which had been shipped from London, had been entirely taken to pieces and part of the shutter was missing. This was probably due to misplaced zeal on the part of some hashish-hunting Customs man. It was a bad blow. We went on and on, sorting and arranging, and I got everything I needed into the office, and told myself that I would unpack it all the next morning, first thing, and get it arranged and organized in the most efficient way possible. Already I'd put in a far longer working day than I'd ever done in London, if you count tramping round an incomprehensible tangle of ruins as work. I do. How nice, I thought, to go to bed early after this first exhausting day.

Tired but gay, we sat down to supper. John was wearing a very fine Cretan cloak, which I was to find was his permanent evening dress at Amarna. It was a soft darkish blue on the outside, embroidered in black braid with a hood folded back, and all lined with scarlet.

Towards the end of the meal he said apologetically to me: "Would you mind very much doing a few letters for me if you can get the typewriter going? I *must* write at once about that camera, and if the boy gets it over the river tonight it will go up to Cairo on the early morning train." 'Strewth, I thought in my low, Bloomsbury way. I got my jaw back into position as quickly as I could so as to murmur "Yes, of course", and tottered into the office, and began ripping open the type-writer carton, and bursting open packets to find headed paper and carbons and a shorthand pad and a pen.

I took down letters to the Customs at Alexandria about the camera, to the Chief of Police asking for guards, to a firm of photographers in Cairo who were going to do our printing, and to the Society to say we had arrived. While I typed them, John talked to Ralph and Hilary about surveying instruments.

65

I slammed away on a table which had been born with one short leg, poor thing, and under a lamp hung in a hopeless position, and felt sorry for myself, and half dead with sleep. Then it occurred to me that John must be rather an unusual person, to be apparently as much at home with cameras and theodolites as he was with date-sequences and hieroglyphs. And if he was going to be a slave-driver, it was already quite obvious to us all who it was that he drove the hardest. A small glow of exhilaration crept across my fatigue. Here was a first chance—at the very outset—of showing that I really intended to play my part in the small team, and not footle about, just getting by, as I had in London.

At about 10 I took the letters over to John for his signature. He read them through in silence, and signed them one by one. Then he called a felucca boy who was waiting outside the office in the moonlight, squatting by the low wall. The boy stuffed all the envelopes into a pouch which hung on his shoulder, and with a smile and a salute slipped off towards the river.

John said: "It's going to save my life having a secretary out here, to cope with all this side of things—we shall be able to do so much more with you taking this off me".

It was exactly what I needed at that very moment. It may have been completely spontaneous as a remark—it may have been a little calculated; the move of a clever leader to win response from the humblest member of the staff by showing how valuable the donkey-work, if well done, could be; it may even have been a bit of both. I don't know. But it put me in a mood now to give the best I had to anything I might be asked to do, however irksome, however tiring.

John got up and said goodnight. "And isn't it wonderful", he said cheerfully, "to think that tomorrow, at last, we *really* begin working."

'*Strewth*, I thought again. But this time I thought it with a grin.

66

Chapter Seven

SUNSHINE and silence again. But as I glanced through the office window when I began work next morning, things looked different. Down over the North Suburb I could see a yellow cloud of dust hanging—the dig had begun.

Hilda and I were staying up at the house for most of the morning and going down to the dig later. I finished arranging files and stationery to my satisfaction and evened up the table leg with a small wedge of wood. Then we arranged the medicine cupboard which stood just inside the office door. Hilda said: "You and I will do it as a rule, but if the others like to as well when there's a mad rush, it's a great help." I looked at her blankly. Then light began to dawn—it certainly had struck me that we had brought a tremendous amount of medical supplies for the possible needs of six people who appeared to be particularly sound of wind and limb. Rather pessimistic, I'd thought.

"What kind of a mad rush?" I asked cautiously.

"Well," she answered, "usually only a few trail up here after the work for treatment—but sometimes they all feel ill at once and then it *is* a mad rush, especially when they have the bright idea of bringing their entire families too. There's no obligation for us to treat more than our own workmen, of course—but it's awfully difficult—impossible really—to refuse the others."

She went off to interview Abd el Latif, and I went on stacking tins of boracic powder and rolls of cotton wool on the shelves. I was depressed. The vision conjured up of the workmen and their wives all feeling ill at once, drooping like dark lilies along our parapet wall, was not inviting. It had been fun

67

watching them detachedly as they came near for their tickets —but I hadn't expected, or wanted, any closer contact; and although some of them looked clear of eye and fairly clean, most of them looked grubby, to say the least, and all of them moved about with a retinue of attentive flies. At that moment an enormous bottle of carbolic which I'd just lugged out of a case, seemed as attractive as if it had been an exotic Parisian perfume. My knowledge of Arabic was still negligible, and of first aid, if possible, less—if I didn't want to depopulate the place it looked as if I had better read up on both subjects pretty smartly.

We set off for the dig. Hilda was the right wife for an archaeologist, for as well as running the domestic side of the dig, she was a classical scholar in her own right, and after marrying John had gone on to extend her work to Cretan and Egyptian archaeology. She told me about their life in Crete where every year they spent the summer months after leaving Egypt. It sounded heavenly. They lived in the Villa Ariadne, close to the Palace of Minos at Knossos, while John carried out his duties as curator.

The very word Crete holds magic; or so it has seemed to me ever since childhood days, when I first heard the story of Theseus and Ariadne and the clew of scarlet thread which brought him safely back to her out of the terrible labyrinth, when he had slain the Minotaur. Later I'd seen pictures of the strange, wonderfully natural Cretan art, the flowers and flying fish painted on the Palace walls, the sea-creatures and water plants curling round the exquisite pottery; and the frescoes showing the athletes in terrible sport, springing and somersaulting over the backs of charging bulls.

But until this morning, I'd never concerned myself with wondering how that detached picture of Crete fitted into the wider historical fabric; and certainly had no idea that there was a possible connection between the lovely art of Crete and the 'new' art of Egypt, which had come to its full flowering during the time of Akhenaten, and in greatest profusion, naturally, at this very spot, his new capital.

We slogged through the sand, while Hilda expounded. Not long before Akhenaten's time, probably in the time of his father, Crete with its great sea-going power had been destroyed, succumbing at last to the growing strength and ambition of the Greek mainland. Knossos and the other cities of the island were left in flames. Perhaps the whole story of Theseus coming from Athens, heroically bearding the Minotaur in his lair, might be a legendary version, even symbolic, of the actual event, sung by the victorious mainlanders down through the centuries. All through history, when the flower of a civilization has been cut down by invasion or revolution, a remnant of its culture has survived, through the escape of artists fleeing before the terror, who bring their music and painting and literature to the countries giving asylum; countries whose great reward is this enrichment. So perhaps Cretan artists too fled south before the storm, to find sanctuary in Egypt when Akhenaten's father was Pharaoh. In exile they painted once again, and the Egyptian artists may have watched their persuasive brushes at work. At any rate, it was just at this time that they began to show this entirely new way of approaching their work. Gone to a great extent were the formal abstractions of pictographic scenes; they began to paint natural objects as if they loved them for their intrinsic beauty, as if they were worth painting for their own sake, not just as rigid details in some pictured story hanging upon an exploit of the Pharaoh. Hilda said there were fragments of frescoes in a Palace at Thebes built by Akhenaten's father, already showing this new kind of painting, plump feathery ducks perfectly drawn, swimming among lotus plants. So that the gentle Akhenaten must have known this kind of painting from boyhood; and how well it coincided with—perhaps even had helped to form—his hatred of militarism, and the ruthlessness of man the hunter, the slayer of bird and beast.

We were about halfway to the dig now. On our right the palms fell back a short way towards the river, and in this sandy bay lay a crumbling tangle of low walls which I had noticed the day before. Already I had seen enough ruined walls to think that it looked more like one very large building than a group of houses.

"The pavement in the Palace down in the south showed some of the finest painting in the new style," Hilda said. "You know Petrie's reproductions of those, don't you?" I said I did, and added, "And then there was the North Palace with the wonderful wall paintings. I've looked at all those marvellous coloured reproductions—but where exactly *was* the North Palace?"

Hilda stopped walking, and laughed.

"Here," she said, and pointed at the tumbled walls close beside us.

"*This* is the North Palace?"

"Yes—didn't you hear John explaining it yesterday as we went by?"

"Out of earshot by that time," I said sadly.

"Yes, I know," she said. "He *does* move, doesn't he?" She explained that although, as I had thought, the main trend of excavation had been steadily from south to north, there had been exceptions; notably the clearing of this North Palace, right up here, not many years before; and a few important buildings further north still.

I thought of the adorable paintings I had looked at in the publication of the North Palace. The soft green marshland plants and flowers painted all round the walls, and in them and above them, hovering and perching among the foliage, softly coloured and yet brilliant, the strange crested birds and pigeons and kingfishers.

All from these sunbaked, crumbling dusty ruins. The pictures in London, and the original walls here—for a moment I tried to bring them together, and see it as it once must have looked —longed to see it—delicate, airy, glittering white against the blue sky, soaring above the trees, while within, the enchanting rooms glowed with their tender lively scenes.

We went on again.

Soon we approached the dig. But we heard it before we rounded a spur of protruding trees and saw it, looking like a newly disturbed anthill. There were occasional shouts, and bursts of strange singing. The work seemed to be in two places. The North Suburb was divided by a dry wadi at one point, which ran at right angles to the river; John had said it might even have been a canal in ancient times so that supplies could come by boat into the heart of the suburb. Most of the workmen, judging by the noise and the dust, were digging beyond this wadi; but a small group of them with about twenty children, and one Gufti in charge, had begun to tackle the south-west corner of the suburb to the north of the wadi. John was there talking to the Gufti, and we joined him.

He told us that the house he had begun lay in square T.34. We stood watching the digging. The sand still filled the rooms to a height of about three feet, so that the work went quickly; for as yet it was a simple matter of clearing down until floor level was nearly reached, where naturally most of the objects —some very fragile—and breakable structures, like steps and ablution slabs and brick benches, would be found. When this stage was reached, the digging would have to go much more cautiously and slowly.

Each tourieh-man would grab an empty rope basket from one or other of his attendant sprites, up-end it against his shins and in half a dozen swift movements of his tourieh draw into it all the sand it would hold. Then the child would pick it up and join the never-ending line of boys and girls moving towards the dump. These dumps had to be carefully sited, not too far from the work and yet not running over any hidden building. The children went to the far end of the dump, spilt their loads down the sloping chute, and quickly came back for more, swinging their baskets now, giggling and singing. Each dump began as a large mound of sand and then stretched out like a long straight dyke a few feet high, towards the desert; with the children running along the top, to and fro, to and fro, on a path beaten flat by their own feet.

It was wonderful how swiftly tons of sand were moved by this primitive method of human co-operation. The rubble seemed to melt away out of the rooms, and the children did not seem to tire. The pattern they made as they wound out of the house, up the dump, round the end and back again had the kind of nonchalant charm of a country dance. The cotton gowns of red and blue and green and orange and white fluttered along the grey-brown dump, the dust flew, and then the girls and boys passed back again into the house, with an occasional shy, brilliant glance up at us as they tossed the empty basket down for the hundredth time on father's toes.

"This is obviously a very fine house," said John with satisfaction. "Look at this." He picked up something lying on the top of a low wall among cardboard boxes and notebooks. It looked to me like a very insignificant column base, just like the ones up at the house, but much smaller. I wondered why that made him think that this was a very fine house.

"It's so much smaller than the ones I've seen," I ventured.

"Exactly," he said. "And whereabouts do you usually find column bases?"

"Well, on the floor, of course," I answered, realizing that I was having an intelligence test.

"Exactly," he said again, "and we're nowhere near the floor of this house yet—a man found it almost as soon as we got the top layer off this morning—about three feet above ground level. What d'you make of that?" He and Hilda looked at me hopefully. I thought desperately. A small column base—but obviously nothing to do with the floor below, or it couldn't have been found where it was. Then I saw.

"Do you mean—could it have belonged to an *upper* floor and fallen through when the house became a ruin?"

"Yes," they said together. "And," John went on, "of course they had much thinner columns and smaller, lighter bases upstairs, so as to put as little pressure as possible on the ceiling of the room below. Ten marks. Come on, let's have lunch."

I felt rather like Alice at the Mad Tea Party. First going through a questionnaire, and then being suddenly invited to lunch in a waste of brick dust—the most unlikely place to find anything to eat. But at that moment old Umbarak appeared. He mounted the highest point of an old dump, holding a whistle; then, making sure that everybody could see him, he slowly drew out from his robes a colossal silver watch. (It was the *best* butter.) He gazed proudly at this for some time—I *think* upside down—and then took a swift unerring glance at the sun. Then he blew the whistle.

The hacking, scraping, shovelling, stopped. The children scampered down the dumps, screaming. The dust settled. The men stretched themselves, getting the kinks out of their spines, and then made their way slowly into the shade, settling down for an hour's rest with little bundles of bread and onions and dates and water-bottles. Tommy and Ralph and Hilary came towards us, looking hot. Another small procession was approaching from the direction of the house—John had seen it five minutes before—two of the big girls who had been taken on to do the water-carrying, laundry and odd jobs, followed by Young Abu Bakr. But whereas he went free of any burden, each girl was balancing on her head a large wooden box.

By the time they arrived, the six of us were sitting in the shade on the ground with our backs against a low wall. The

73

girls yanked the boxes off their heads, laid them at our feet and retired giggling. Abu Bakr carefully unpacked and handed round the contents of one —a plate (hot), glass, fork, bread, even a paper napkin. The other box yielded an enormous cottage pie, still piping hot even after its long journey from the house. I looked inside the box afterwards and saw that there wasn't much Abd el Latif didn't know about the principle of haybox  cookery. It was stuffed full of straw and tightly rolled wads of newspaper with a neat nest in the middle just big enough to jam the pie-dish into. He would have made a wonderful member of the Women's Institute.

Abu Bakr served us alertly, and although almost standing on his head to reach us on the ground, contrived to invest the proceedings with the dignity of luncheon at the Guildhall. We followed up the pie with fruit and chocolate and lemonade and cigarettes, and then talked peacefully while Abu Bakr packed up, summoned his underlings and marched them off back to the house.

It was a jolly moment—just to lean back in the warm, sunny  air against the ancient house wall, and listen. Ralph and Hilary had been setting up surveying posts most of the morning, with young Kassar Umbarak to help. They both agreed that he was very bright and quick, considering that neither of them knew enough Arabic to explain things to him. "Quicker you do, the better," said John with his eyes shut. Tommy had been overseeing the dig beyond the wadi, but he had no inscriptions to work on as yet. John said he would make a quick round of the rest of the work just before knocking-off time, but that he intended to spend most of the afternoon near the big house.

"What's the name of it called?" asked Ralph, who knew the classics. John laughed, and said, "T.34.1."

Then old Umbarak blew his whistle. And soon the dust was flying again and the children running. Hilda and I went back to the house, and had hardly sat down when Hussein shimmered in, rather in the manner of Jeeves, with a cup of tea. It was just as well, for when the others arrived later, parched and grey with dust, clamouring for tea, Hilda and I were ready for the casualties, five in number, who had come up too. I went out nervously to the medicine cupboard. Between us we dealt with a small cut, a bruised nose, a boil, and two cases of pink eye, both children; they seemed to get it more than the adults, I found. At first pink eye made me feel sick and nothing else—eyelids badly swollen and red, the eye closed and discharging, and the eyeball, if you could manage to see it at all, very bloodshot. Our only treatment for it was to bathe the eyes in warm boracic water, and if possible get some of the solution under the lids with a dropper, and then send the patient off with a little boracic and cotton wool, and explain that he must bathe it again several times before the next day's treatment at the house. At first it seemed hopelessly inadequate treatment to me, but I found after a bit that the children mostly reacted extraordinarily quickly to this simple piece of hygiene. Sometimes a child would appear at the wall, grinning all over, pointing to his wide-open eyes, the whites shining, the iris dark and brilliant; I would wonder if I'd ever seen him before, and then suddenly recognize the miserable waif, whimpering with discomfort, who had been led up to me two or three days ago, eyes closed and swollen. Most of them were so healthy—you needed to be to survive babyhood in an Egyptian village—that the mild germicidal treatment had this almost instantaneous effect. This was encouraging—and later I became so interested in the individual cases and their progress, that I quite got over the first squeamishness, in trying to get them to understand how to keep cured, how to keep further infection at bay from the start by a few simple rules of cleanliness.

But on that first evening I felt nothing but disgust for their condition, mixed with pity. I went off to my room armed with carbolic and a gargle, and used them both before doing anything else. There was a flat round tin bath on the floor, and an enormous can of hot water beside it; and having bathed the dusty day away, I cheered up again.

As soon as the table was cleared after supper, I was initiated into the mysteries of Registration, for already on this first day a few objects had been found. They probably came from upper rooms like the little column base, because they had been picked out of the sand well above floor level, which had not yet been reached anywhere.

They were laid on the table under the lamp, each resting on a piece of paper which gave the exact locus where it had been found. Among them was a small stone, carved in the shape of a duck, which John said was a weight; two bronze needles with the eyes still intact; part of a bronze blade; and a few coloured beads and amulets. I was soon to get used to that sight, evening after evening; but at first it was a most curious feeling to pick up and handle things which, until that day, had not been touched since some subject of Akhenaten— who had probably quite often watched the Pharaoh and his lady, Nefertiti, and their children driving by in their informal way—had handled them, and then dropped and lost them.

There was a pile of large square cards on the table, printed at the top 'Tell el Amarna'; they were lined in centimetre squares, and subdivided into millimetre squares, so that it was easy to make scale-drawings on them. Each individual object was entered on one of these cards. Here was shown the date it was found, its serial number, a short description, its exact find-spot, its measurements, material, and a scale-drawing—but actual size if it could be fitted in—any relevant remarks,  and later on, its negative number. There was need for great accuracy here, for these cards were the sole records containing all the information needed for the final publication of the objects.

The same scheme was followed for any new or particularly interesting types of beads, amulets, ring bezels or clay sealings. But for the great majority of small objects such as these, which were mass-produced in clay moulds in their thousands, a different method of registration was used; for obviously it would have been a quite impracticable labour to make a card for each of them. Yet it was necessary to record their details equally carefully somehow, for their value as evidence was important, though in a different way from the more individual objects. This was particularly so in the case of the ring bezels, which often bore a Royal name. The smallest piece of evidence is of course important to the good field archaeologist, and is weighed in with the main body of evidence which is pointing him to certain conclusions. One isolated faience ring bezel of gleaming yellow or green or blue can tell him nothing, however pretty it is. But if, on adding up the numbers of Royal names on ring bezels, and their find-spots, he finds that in one part of the dig, one Royal name appears in far greater numbers than any other, and that perhaps in another part of the dig the balance is the other way, he is given furiously to think, as I will show. The mass-produced objects, in their humble way, thus yielded their own very useful evidence, based on statistics. The principle of recording these had been devised by Petrie, and generally adopted with variations and modifications, and was entirely effective with very little time and labour involved.

Our own method was this: John had already pinned across the wall opposite where we sat at the long table, great sheets of diagrams in black ink. There were two showing sections of pottery, inside and out; another for beads, each bead drawn sideways as well as in section, in a bewildering variety of shapes and sizes; one for amulets; and one for ring bezels. Each of these had a type number, sub-divided to show variations, printed below it. When a bead or amulet or bezel came up for registration, we looked for its type on the sheet first, and if it were there, simply noted in a special book that a bead of type so-and-so was found in such-and-such a room. That was all—no card; and the beads were then sorted into boxes to be made up at our leisure [*sic*] into strings and necklaces. If its type didn't appear on the sheet, that is to say, if nothing like it had ever been found before, it attained to the dignity of a card all to itself, as I have said, as well as having its portrait added to the sheet on the wall; for then, of course, it was no longer a new type.

The faience beads and amulets and ring bezels were made in clay moulds, which were often found, the finger marks of the ancient moulder often still showing where he had pressed the soft clay round the first object to be copied. Metal objects were cast in stone moulds which could stand up to much greater heat in the firing.

This first registration was short, for the objects were few. John and Hilda did the typing of the beads and amulets, while Tommy and I did the cards. Tommy kept saying he couldn't draw anyway, and it was no good asking him to; and ended the session by turning out miracles of neatness and accuracy by keeping close to the millimetre squares, and measuring every possible dimension of his objects; while I, who rather fancied my draughtsmanship, was told to hold on to myself and never mind about art. It was great fun to be putting on record the very first finds of our new season. When I thought we'd finished, Tommy said, "Well, now of course you have to mark the objects themselves with the serial numbers you've put on the cards," and showed me how it was done. This also needed care, because the number must be put on clearly, in permanent ink, and yet in an inconspicuous place, so as not to spoil its looks. The very small objects had tiny boxes with the number on the lid, or, if they could be fixed without danger of coming adrift, tiny tag labels, which were fiddly to do. At last we carried them carefully into the antiquity room behind us, and arranged them neatly at the end of one shelf. I think those first few finds made the rest of the shelf space look emptier than before—but I was terribly proud of them.

We swept the dust and sand off the table, and John said in the style of Pharaoh: "My Majesty requires beer." Beer arrived, followed wonderfully closely by Ralph and Hilary, who had been in the drawing-office. We all had some. There was a good feeling of a settled routine getting under way, with this cheerful coming together at the end of a long day's work again. John was doodling comfortably at the back of a notebook while he talked—from where I was sitting it looked like a quartered shield with a crest consisting of a Gufti's head.

"This is a shield for the dig," he said. "I've got crossed touriehs 1st and 4th quarterly. What shall I have 2nd and 3rd?"

"A little basket," said Ralph promptly, who came from Chelsea.

John smiled gently without looking up, and put in a little

basket, 2nd and 3rd quarterly. Then he drew a beautiful empty scroll under the shield. "Now what about a motto?"

Modesty prevents me from mentioning who said, "Infra dig," but I still think it was rather good on the spur of the moment.

John smiled again, and carefully printed it in.

Chapter Eight

THE dig was in full swing—and the pace was quickening. In spite of violent protest Ralph and Hilary and Tommy were gradually disappearing behind three rather horrid beards. They said it saved a lot of time in the morning—but one noticed that John remained scrupulously shaven, and yet still seemed to do more work than anyone else.

He did all the photography—usually considered a whole-time job on digs—which meant not only the work of recording every important and significant architectural feature on the dig itself, but also getting an absolutely clear photograph of every object as well. The quality, not to mention the usefulness, of a dig publication can be very much reduced by fuzzy pictures (and unfortunately often is), and whatever method is used for reproduction, on however good paper, whether by half-tone or collotype or what-have-you, some sharpness is bound to be lost in the process. So of course the maximum degree of clarity is essential in the original print. John used to spread a black cloth on one of the column bases in the courtyard and arrange the objects on that, fixing the tripod so that the camera was focused vertically over them. He did all the developing himself in the aforementioned evil cubbyhole of a dark-room. We sent the negatives—half-plate film-pack—to Cairo for printing, and although it was possible to get some idea of the quality of the photograph from the negative, it was an exciting moment when the parcel came back and we saw the finished prints for the first time. When they had been passed as satisfactory, I took them over into my department for filing and cross-referencing; the appropriate negative number had to go on the object cards, and the object numbers had to go on the negatives and prints. Many of the small objects were photographed on one plate, in a group, just because of their similarity, and for this very reason a lot of care had to be taken, by comparing the cards with the prints, to be quite sure I had got the right number with each object; for the number was often marked on the back or side of the actual object, and so was concealed in the photograph. I soon found out how important it was to draw the measurements accurately on the cards; sometimes it was the only clue for sorting out, say, a row of almost identical bronze fishhooks or knife blades on a print.

The object numbers were written on the back of each of three copies of the prints in the appropriate spot, rather in the manner of the holiday snapshot sent to loving relatives, and nearly as hard to work out as you flip it back and forth: 'Jim, Jim's friend (see my letter), Mrs. Peabody, Self, Johnny (in white hat), Fred (with Ginger), and Pam (she moved).' When there was a large group of nearly identical objects close together on a plate, it was a laborious business and took a good deal of office time. It made clearer than ever why, without one person on the staff dedicated to this side of the work, the records had hitherto arrived in the office in such a wild state, with the specialists somehow cramming these details into their working day.

My days were usually filled with office details of this kind; then there were accounts to do, and letters and reports to type, and objects to clean and perhaps mend. Sometimes I never got down to the dig at all for a day or two. I would look up from the typewriter through the window and see the yellow haze which always hung over the dig, and wish I were down there —sometimes, perversely, I might be happily slogging through a pile of prints, aware that I could polish them off before lunch if I kept at it, when there would be an unwelcome interruption; a message from the dig that I was wanted down there, and I would know that the job in hand would have to be shelved until after the evening's registration if it were to be finished the same day.

When something fragile was found, needing infinite care (and therefore time) and a light touch in handling, an appeal usually came up to the house, and either Hilda or I, or both of us if we could, went down to the dig. The Guftis were very clever at this work, but there wasn't always a Gufti available if delicate finds were turning up in more than one place at once.

It was one of those days. I was unscrambling the shorthand notes for the first report which John was sending to a London paper, when a shadow fell across the doorway behind me. Young Kassar Umbarak had run up from the dig with a note —although it was quite a mile, and a hot day, he wasn't even sweating. He stood there poised for the return flight, lithe and gay, his dark face alert. 'I think we've found a necklace,' said the note, 'can you come and deal with it, please?' Kassar flew off to say that I was on the way, and I collected a small drawing-board, pencils, brushes, tweezers, a knife, sun-glasses and a hat, waved farewell to the office, and set out, grumbling mildly, into the glare. When should I get at that report again? But as soon as I was on my way I began to think that it was rather a lark to be an odd-job person of this kind, slapping away at a typewriter one moment, and digging up ancient necklaces the next.

The house with the find had been cleared, except for a heap of rubble up against one low wall. Already some faience rings had been found in the heap, one bearing the cartouche of Nefertiti; and there were glazed beads to be seen here and there on the surface. And here, said John, pointing, was obviously the main part of a necklace to which most of these fragments probably belonged. Would I cope, while he moved the team to the next house? I said I would, took one look at the problem before me, and knew for a fact that the report, far away on my desk, would *not* be ready before nightfall.

83

Necklaces were tricky because the threads had worn away, so that each pendant had to be lifted separately; and if a necklace had fallen in a heap before being buried, it was sometimes impossible to be sure that we reconstructed the pattern correctly. Today we were lucky. I began by blowing away the surface sand very gently from the topmost beads—following the technique perfected by the Guftis, whom by now I had sometimes watched at just this kind of work. Through the thin veil of sand gleamed fragments of red and yellow and green and white. I brushed very lightly and then blew again—and there, lying on the sand, just as it had fallen more than three thousand years ago, was the main part of the necklace—a confused heap of beads at one end, to be sure, but happily a stretch of at least three inches lying quite flat, enough to show the pattern. The thread had perished, of course, but pendants and beads were lying exactly as if still threaded, in a fan-shape of three rows. If I were breathlessly careful, I could save this tiny piece of archaeological knowledge.

All the pendants were fashioned like fruit and flowers—there were enchanting white daisies, blue grape-clusters, mauve-tipped lotus petals, and rust-red pomegranates. Here it was again, this delight of Akhenaten's people in the beautiful simplicity of natural design and colour. I suddenly remembered, sitting back on my heels and gazing at it, a bead necklace I'd had as a little girl, which had completely fascinated me—small white daisies, yellow-hearted, linked together by fragile strings of tiny green beads. I felt sure that this necklace, too, had belonged to someone rather young, someone who had felt the same delight at wearing the pretty thing over her best white frock. I'd often wondered how the people of Amarna managed to lose so many of their possessions, as we picked up one thing after another out of the heaps of rubble—but after all, where was *my* daisy necklace now? Would some strange Wellsian creature, three thousand years hence, digging for history beneath the grassy mounds covering London, down through the collapsed rubbish that had once been Bloomsbury, come upon it, and finger it gently, and find it somehow pathetic?

But daydreams were a menace to neat field-work. I snapped out of it, and began to concentrate on the business of salvaging the necklace in good order. I made a diagram-drawing of the whole pattern on the drawing-board, writing in notes about the colour scheme, for some of the pendants were the same shape, but coloured differently. Then I began raising each pendant and small bead with tweezers, laying them out on the board beside the diagram in the correct order. This would save time when it came to rethreading the whole thing; but I still might need the drawing, for in the event of the necklace getting joggled out of position on its journey up to the house, or even by some misfortune spilled completely, it could still be correctly put together again by means of the diagram.

I spent the afternoon working through the heap of rubble, picking up loose pendants which belonged to the necklace; the pace had to be slow, in case of disturbing yet another stretch of beads, perhaps made up in a different way; one ruthless jab with a knife into the rubble might bring down a shower of earth, and with it a stream of beads and pendants, carrying with them the secret of their shattered pattern, lost for ever. There was no such necklace, as it turned out, but I found one thing that belonged to the original one—a small flat triangular piece of cream-coloured faience, decorated with a small curving lotus flower in mauve and green. It had one hole pierced through at the apex and three close together along the opposite side. It was one of the two end-pieces of the necklace, each of its rows having once been fastened to one of the three holes; and the necklace must have been joined behind the neck by some kind of fastening, perhaps a thin cord, threaded through the hole in the apex of each end-piece.

At the end of the afternoon Kassar and another young Gufti

carried the board up to the house without shifting a bead, and keeping perfectly calm; which was wonderful, really, as they had me nervously circling round them the whole way, rather in the manner of a cow with a new-born calf. They laid the whole thing in the antiquity room to await registration, and then trotted off to their evening meal. I had never felt grittier and sandier—or more elated. I asked Young Abu Bakr to bring a 'tisht' (a flat tin bath, according to the manual) to my room as soon as he could. He went off to get it, respectful as ever, but with a sudden wild grimace which I had noticed before at the same request. It looked curiously like a hastily— but not quite hastily enough—concealed chortle. Once again looking the soul of decorum, he brought the 'tisht' and lots of hot water, and retired; and it wasn't for weeks more that I learned that in his part of the country 'tisht' meant frying-pan.

That was one difficulty in learning the language. The Egyptians were too polite to tell you when you went wrong; so long as they grasped your meaning, they would make no comment or correction, in fact even cheerfully use the wrong word back at you rather than upset you. Or perhaps, it wasn't so much politeness with these simple souls, as reluctance to end a good joke. I must have brightened life considerably for the Abu Bakr family while I was at Amarna. I can imagine Young Abu Bakr going back to the kitchen evening after evening and reporting to Uncle Abd el Latif that the lady was taking her bath in the frying-pan again, and Uncle doubling up in stitches every time, as he stirred the soup for the evening meal.

There was time before supper that evening to have a look at the bronzes which I was helping to clean. We had a large developing dish full of acid—Rochelle Salts mostly—on the table in the second little inner room, and the encrusted bronze finds lay in it for days, gradually losing the beautiful blue-green patina of the centuries and revealing again their original dark brown sharp-edged shapes. There were heavy hoe-heads, not unlike our modern touriehs, axe-heads, blades of all kinds, scale-pans, weights, an occasional fine ring, fishhooks and needles, tweezers and scissors and tongs. I brushed at them every day gently, hoping for an inscription on handle or bezel to gladden the heart of the inscription-panting Tommy. One or two of the ring bezels had one form or the other of Akhenaten's titles cut into them. His official cognomen was 'Nefer-kheperu-ra Wa-en-ra' (Beautiful are the forms of Ra, the Unique one of Ra); his own name, Akhenaten, meaning 'It is well with the Aten[1]:

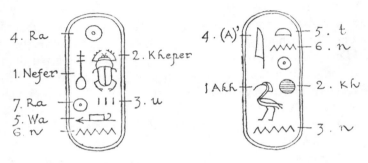

How these meanings developed from the tiny pictures of beetles and sun disks and birds and water—the whole development of hieroglyphs in fact—first as single phonetic sounds, and then grouped together, to express such abstract ideas as truth and beauty and strength and existence, has been a completely absorbing study to philologists ever since the Rosetta Stone yielded the first clue; for myself, I only gleaned enough of the phonetic sounds and meanings to be able to read the few Royal names which turned up in connection with the site of Amarna; but even that—to be able to puzzle out the names from the hieroglyphic signs—was fascinating.

I would have liked to believe that these inscribed bronze rings had actually belonged to Akhenaten himself—but they

87

had been found in houses in the North Suburb, and were much more likely to have belonged to citizens who showed their loyalty in this way.

Also sitting in the acid bath was a charming bronze frog, with a small ring in his back to take a chain; he looked quite at home in this unusual sort of pond, as he quietly reverted from bright green to sombre brown. There were other amulets of animals; ducks and part of a crocodile. It was natural that water-birds and river-animals appeared so often; the river was so intrinsic a part of life in Egypt, ever present in the minds of the people; consciously as a great waterway, and supplier of fish and water-fowl and game for the table; unconsciously, perhaps, as the very source of life, as its rich water flowed inland along the channels cut between the gardens and allotments.

Even this little group of bronzes by itself, unconnected with our other finds, gave a powerful glimpse into the vanished everyday life of Akhenaten's people. I think I was lucky in coming to Amarna the way I did—for in one sense, perhaps, my greenness gave me one small but definite advantage over the professionals; everything that happened had the quality of a small electric shock, for I didn't know enough about anything beforehand to take anything for granted. There was no padding, no insulation, made up of familiarity, to deaden the shoot of delight that I felt at touching even the poorest of the little everyday things we found; and this gave to them a vividness that made me feel as if I had not only travelled to Akhenaten's capital across space, but through time as well.

I think this odd feeling of time folding up into nothing was intensified by the knowledge that the very rooms we worked and lived in—the little room I was musing in now—had been 'Their' rooms too. They had passed in and out of this same doorway into the living-room. It seemed as likely as not that instead of Hussein coming to bid me to supper, another might appear framed in the dark doorway; a man with thick dusky hair bound with a fillet, wearing a white pleated skirt, bracelets clipped above bare elbows, sandals on his feet.

I was coming at it all the wrong way round, professionally speaking; practical work first, and 'looking it up' afterwards. But for me, as an amateur, it was very much the right way round. The handling of the possessions of the simple people made me really want to know more about *their* lives in the first place, and then, perhaps, but less urgently, something more about the great ones, the rulers, and their effect on history in a wider, more abstract way.

It's all come so suddenly alive from the start, I found myself thinking. Some of these bronzes that I'm brushing at now came in on the first day of digging—and now, too, there is today's enchanting necklace. Three thousand years hasn't done much to alter domestic needs and fancies, nor the skill in shaping the same sort of objects to meet them. Perhaps when I move into the living-room, it may look different—strangers may be sitting along a cushioned dais, where our rickety divan should be, eating fruit from a high golden stand. Perhaps, there may be a girl sitting by a brazier, her small brown hand guiding these twisted scissors (which just now I fished up out of the acid) round a carefully pinned piece of white linen. I think it's to be a new gown for a ceremony in the Temple, or at the Window of Appearances, when Pharaoh will honour one of his faithful servants with presents of gold. I seem to see the girl cutting it out, lightly frowning in concentration, delicate eyebrows plucked to a thin, springing line with the little tweezers now soaking in the acid. Perhaps those shining needles in a padded work-box at her side are the same green-encrusted ones that I have just been handling. A man sitting near takes up some tongs (surely I know them?) and adds a little fuel to the brazier, and then picks up a box full of wicked little gleaming fishhooks—the very same which I was just now gingerly brushing—and begins to fashion a trawl-line. And as he works a little frog amulet hanging on a polished chain round his neck, winks and twinkles in the firelight. They are all talking quietly, and laughing a little; friendly people.

There *is* a murmur of voices and a step in the next room; a beam of light moving round the dusky walls interrupts my daydream; and glancing round I find, after all, that I'm rather glad that it is smiling old Hussein hanging the lamp above the solid supper table.

I slid all the bronzes back into the solution, and went through into the warm, familiar living-room. And it had its usual look of the island hut in *The Admirable Crichton*—the mats on the sandy floor, the wooden stools and camp-chairs, the rough wooden pillars supporting the ceiling; and through the wide doorway the glimpse of palms and cliffs and an occasional gleam of silver water.

Hilary was at the door talking to the half-wild dog which he had tamed. He had a deep feeling for animals—rather too deep sometimes, when a needed plan was still on his drawing-board, and Hilary was to be found in raptures over a lizard clinging to the wall, which he was examining with the aid of an electric torch and a magnifying glass. But I think he was the only one of us who hadn't felt uncomfortable when this woolly-coated, yet hungry, wolf-like brute had rushed at us from the cultivation, snarling and growling, soon after our arrival. Day after day he all but attacked us; but Hilary couldn't rest till he had made friends. By soft words, and small pieces of food, and much patience, he gradually won him, first to a distrustful silence; then to a kind of shame-faced slinking oblique approach, as he sniffed yearningly round a proffered tit-bit. Then one day Hilary's hand rested on the rough head unresented, while he wolfed down scraps thrown on the ground; and at last came the complete surrender; a shaggy muzzle laid on his knee, and a shaggy tail moving clumsily in a most unaccustomed gesture of goodwill.

After that he came quietly up to the house, and became a very fine watch-dog. In honour of the well-known archaeologist, who had himself worked at Amarna after the first World War for some years, Hilary called him Leonard because he was so woolly. One of my happier moments was hearing Hilary, with the only half-dozen words of Arabic which he was ever known to use, trying to explain this joke to Hussein, who of course remembered Sir Leonard Woolley too. Somehow, I don't think it got across, although Hussein did his best and laughed like anything.

The talk at supper was of T.34.1. It was living up to the expectation that it would turn out an interesting house; for a fine doorway, framed in red-painted stone, had been discovered late that afternoon, at the end of a passage leading to the rooms to the west side of it. Both the jambs and the lintel had fallen back into the passage, collapsing when the mud walls had crumbled; but although one jamb was broken in one or two places, the whole thing was there.

"I'm going to have it rebuilt back in position tomorrow," said John. "It's unusual to find the whole thing like this; and all the thresholds of the other doorways are stone too—and we haven't cleared the main door into the Central Room yet; that might be even finer."

The next morning all of us who could assembled in T.34.1, and watched the raising of the heavy red jambs. The broken pieces were cemented together; and at last the heavy lintel, its cornice curved at the top, was hauled up on ropes and eased into position by Guftis standing on a rough scaffolding of planks and boxes. Until the cement should be thoroughly dry, battens of wood were fixed across, front and back, for extra support; but the old doorway hardly seemed to need it— sturdy yet graceful it stood in place once again, six feet in height, and although undecorated except for the red coat of paint, it looked very good.

Then John gave orders for the walls on either side of it to be built up to the same height as the lintel for a few feet either way, partly as support and partly to make a more realistic setting. While this was going on a man came across from the northern side of the house, where Tommy was in charge of the men clearing the main doorway which led from the north vestibule to the great Central Room. Would the Mudir come and look, please? The Mudir would, and did; and we followed after.

The sand had been cleared down to ground level. Right across the outside of the doorway lay a great oblong of limestone, quite seven feet long by about three feet wide. It was far too big and rough to be a doorstep, and in any case, this was not the outer wall of the house.

"Another lintel, I think," said John. "Fallen on its face. Perhaps the other side is painted too."

It must have weighed several hundredweights. Four short poles were found, and these were worked very carefully under the outer long side. Sweating and straining, four of the workmen began to raise the outer edge inch by inch, pivoting it up on the inner edge. Stones were slipped in to hold it when they paused for breath or to work the levers further in. A few chunks of limestone, cracked probably in the first crash when the lintel fell, broke away from the edges and lay in the sand. Would the whole thing crack to pieces as the great weight left the support of the ground?

At a word from Ali Sheraif, the Gufti in charge, the men bent to the poles again, marvellously slow and careful, grunting to each other words of warning. We were all in it together somehow. They were just as keen to get it up intact as we were —and I am perfectly certain it wasn't only the prospect of good baksheesh ahead. As for us, we stood round in a sort of desperate tension of silence. When the front edge was about six inches off the ground and more supports had been wedged in, Tommy slid his long length alongside and got as much of his head as he could into the narrow space.

" Are those supports all right?" Hilda murmured uncomfortably.

A strangled, very sandy "*Gosh!*" floated up from the depths.

"Is there—anything?" asked John, moving about anxiously.

Tommy withdrew his head and, with maddening deliberation, folded himself up again, rather like a camel, behind first, until he was sitting back on his heels, looking up at us. His countenance, sunburned by now to a rich tomato, was beaming, and his spectacles flashed in the sun.

"It's covered in bright colours," he said, in rather a shaky voice, and then, bringing out his trump card: "—and simply smothered in inscriptions!"

John, Ralph and Hilary held a meeting very suddenly under the edge of the lintel. Hilda and I decided to wait until we could look at it from a rather more flattering angle. The workmen realized that something extra good was coming up, and began to laugh and sing. Ali Sheraif, the perfect N.C.O. as always, although deeply thrilled, remained calm, and began to direct raising operations again.

At last the great lintel was upright, and then very gently the men eased it back an inch or two until it was leaning across the base of the doorway it had once crowned, supported by the walls on either side.

It was a wonderful moment. So much of the digging and so many of the finds produced evidence which at best could only be interpreted by intelligent conjecture, lacking definite proof. But with an inscription it was different. Here was a concrete statement, directly intended as information in the first place. It was like a clear voice ringing out above a mass of half-heard, half-guessed-at murmurs.

We all sat round it at lunch-time while Tommy and John worked through the inscriptions. The great curved cornice was gaily painted in vertical bands of red and green and blue. Although the top edge was badly broken, all the pieces were there on the ground, and it was obvious that a little cement work was all that was needed to make the whole thing as good as new.

Below the cornice, running the whole width of the lintel was a rounded moulding, painted yellow and decorated with a blue design, which looked like a ribbon twisted along it. Below that came three distinct panels. The centre one, twice the size of either of the outer ones, contained ten cartouches, four very large ones in the centre, and three smaller on either side. The four large cartouches held the names of the Aten; the three on either side matched each other, Nefertiti's name appearing on the single one at either end, and Akhenaten's double cartouches between these and the four large central ones. I say Nefertiti's name and Akhenaten's cartouches purposely, for his own names were no longer there—they had been carefully and completely chipped away in antiquity. I knew, of course, that his religious ideas had ended by bringing violence and bitter hatred against him—but this was the first time that I had seen concrete evidence of that hate. The heretic name had been wiped out; yet his consort's name, that of the lovely lady who had stood by him and championed all his revolutionary ideas, had here been left inviolate. What reason could there be for this differentiation between the Royal couple? Here was a fresh query to pitch at the heads of my patient mentors.

All the central panel was conventional enough. But the smaller side panels were personal and, therefore, more interesting. On either side, each facing the centre panel, knelt a man with upraised arms—beautifully drawn and cut and painted—worshipping the Royal and Divine names of the Aten. Above each figure were six short columns of hieroglyphs, and it was these that gave us the name and business of the very owner and builder of T.34.1. His name was Hatiay, and he was of some importance, for the inscription stated that he was Overseer of Works. And very nice too. A man in his position was well placed to secure such magnificent stone thresholds, such stone jambs and great lintels.

After the midday break, work began on the business of carrying the lintel up to the house. Somehow the contraption for this didn't seem to be thought out by anybody—we had noticed before, that whenever some apparently unprecedented problem of man-handling had to be got round, the solution was already there, not suggested by any one Gufti or workman rather brighter than the others, but as if they all knew about it, as the normal way to get something done. It never involved the use of wheels. It was always done by a combined and carefully contrived distribution of man-power, completely simple, and yet astonishingly effective.

Nowadays, in progressive countries, men beat their brains out working on scientific formulae concerning strains and stresses and pressure points, in order to achieve the best way of shifting heavy weights about in industry. Lacking such aids to efficiency, the country folk of Egypt in their own primitive way, nevertheless, seemed to understand instinctively all the scientific principles for getting a heavy job done with the least waste of energy. As they hadn't heard the news about weight-distribution, and centres of gravity and such, how did they come to act exactly as if they had? The only other way they could have reached such a pitch of simple efficiency was by an inherited experience forged from a process of trial and error which had been perfected unknown ages ago. I am sure the truth of it was that the inborn knowledge of these peasants came down to them through six thousand years or so, from the days when the scale of building in Egypt first began to need just such skill in lifting and transporting great pieces of stone.

I think we were watching something rather wonderful that

afternoon, for all its rough simplicity—something was animating these brown agile men, a stirring in their blood-stream as they turned themselves into a machine of flesh and bone which harked back to their fathers of the dim, gigantic past, to the men who also had sweated together to shift the great stone blocks down on sledges and rollers from quarries east of the river, then westward by raft over the river towards the plains, where the first great pyramid-tombs and temples of Pharaoh were slowly rising up out of the sand, black against the sunset.

Our men knew exactly and immediately how to get the lintel up to the house. For us, dependent on the idea of the wheel, and entirely lacking any kind of wheel on that side of the river, the problem would have required a good deal of thought and experiment. All that happened, however, was that poles were tied together until there were four very long ones, each about fifteen feet. These were arranged as if a giant were going to play a game of noughts-and-crosses, and lashed very firmly. The centre square was made a little smaller than the area of the lintel itself. Then the great cross was brought along until the ends of the upper pair of arms touched the lintel; and it wasn't long before the lintel itself had been trundled carefully along these two wooden rails by means of three short poles acting as rollers; as one roller was passed over, it was taken round to the front and laid under the lintel again. Soon the great stone was resting on canvas pads spread over the centre crossing; and roped lightly for security. And then about forty men—five or so to each of the eight projecting pole ends— lifted the whole thing to their shoulders as if it were a feather. It sounds in the telling to be a very simple and obvious idea; but I doubt very much if anyone reading this, faced with the same problem, could have thought quickly of anything at once so simple and so practical, which got so many men so close to the central weight.

John set out swiftly ahead of them to be at the house when the lintel was unloaded. Ali Sheraif gave the word, and the company moved off after him, and coming up with him, remained a few feet behind all the way. Whether by accident or charming design on the part of Ali, it looked exactly like a small military formation with the undoubted leader at its head. Not only looked, but indeed was so—the company-commander was leading his men home with the spoils of victory, with his trusted N.C.O., Ali Sheraif, alongside the company.

There was a look about John's retreating back as if he were full of elation and pride—and so, indeed, he told us later, he had felt.

Soon they were hidden in the cloud of dust which their passing had raised, but we heard Ali Sheraif begin an improvised song of praise, in honour of the good day, and of the splendid find which they were carrying up to the house. The men shouted a refrain which helped to mark the rhythm of their march. You might call it a sand-chanty, for it was the exact equivalent of the sailor's working song; first a narrating soloist cheering the work along, and then the hearty response. John told us afterwards that the chorus ran: "*W'Allah* ne*gib*! *W'Allah* ne*gib*!" beaten out in time to their footsteps. "By *God*! We're *bring*ing it along! By *God*! We're *bring*ing it along!" Over and over again.

By the time the rest of us got back that evening, the lintel was leaning against the inner courtyard wall, covered up in sacking. All was quiet again, and a good day was drawing to its close.

The season was not yet half-way through, but already there were good results to report. Perhaps we might begin to hope that that good-humoured shouted refrain could apply equally well to the season as a whole. Perhaps we too could sing with truth: 'W'Allah negib! W'Allah negib!'

97

Chapter Nine

AFTER the registration one evening, when ring bezels had appeared with the name of Smenkhkare several times, I asked Tommy if he would do me a kindness, and unscramble the ramifications of Akhenaten's family for me, once and for all.

"There isn't a once and for all," he said. "All we can do is to build up a family relationship which will fit the known facts, about how they actually referred to one another, and where that is uncertain, fit in the rest from what we know about dates and length of lives and reigns. New evidence might easily upset the apple cart any day—but until it does there's nothing to show that what we think now isn't right. Most people would agree with John's suggested family-tree—and it's very likely the true one."

"What and who is Smenkhkare, and where does he come in?"

"Akhenaten's father," said Tommy patiently, "was Amenhotep III."

"I know," I said humbly, "but Smenkhkare——"

"Akhenaten's father," Tommy repeated, beginning to look like an interrupted Professor, "was Amenhotep III."

I said nothing.

"His children," he went on amiably, "were certainly Akhenaten and Nefertiti; probably Smenkhkare, and even possibly Tutankhaten, who could have been three years old when Amenhotep died. There was also another daughter, Sitamun, who *may* even have been Smenkhkare's and Tutankhaten's mother as well as their half-sister."

I said I knew that Akhenaten and Nefertiti were probably brother and sister.

"Well, you know they had six daughters," Tommy said, "in the order—Meritaten, Maketaten, Ankhsenpaaten, Neferneferuaten, Neferneferure and Setepenre. We don't know much about the three youngest except that they appear every now and then in the family paintings. But of the others, the eldest married her young half-uncle, Smenkhkare; the next, Maketaten, died young; and Ankhsenpaaten married her even younger half-uncle, Tutankhaten."

Ralph was beginning to listen. He was making a first sketch for a reconstruction of Hatiay's house. "What was Smenkhkare's importance? Why does his name turn up on rings and suchlike?"

"He was co-opted on to Akhenaten's throne on his marriage to Akhenaten's daughter," Tommy replied.

"Why?" asked Hilary, who was trying to make his pet lizard drink beer through a straw.

Tommy appeared surprised but gratified at his growing class. "Well it was quite a normal thing for Pharaoh to do when his heir was growing up—and Smenkhkare's claim to the throne was made valid by his marriage to the King's daughter. But in this case I think there was a special reason for the co-option coming when it did."

I slid a pale-blue faience ring, bearing Smenkhkare's name, on my finger. We had found it that day, and it had just been labelled.

Tommy went on. "You know the Amarna tablets showed that because Akhenaten had no interest in militarism, or in keeping a firm hand on hostile elements beyond his borders, or even in sending reinforcements to his loyal vassals, the Empire was crumbling at the edges?"

We said we did.

"Well, the idea is that to begin with Akhenaten and Nefertiti were completely at one in their attitude towards the priests of Amun and the old religion, and also in their new ideals about

living for beauty and living in truth. But although Nefertiti remained a fanatic on the subject till her dying day, it looks very much as if Akhenaten, not long before he died, saw that things were getting so bad on the frontiers—not to mention internally as well—that if he was to survive as Pharaoh at all, he must give way a little, compromise a bit, patch it up some-how with the big men at Thebes."

"D'you think he was actually disillusioned about his own ideas himself by that time?" asked Ralph, sketching in a miniature lintel over Hatiay's door. "You're making that lizard as oiled as a newt, Hilary."

"You can't say," said Tommy. "All you can be fairly sure about is that he had the wit to see that he wasn't able, even as

Pharaoh, to impose and diffuse his ideas all through the Empire, as I suppose he'd thought at first he could. It's fairly certain that this caused a split between him and Nefertiti. And the action he took probably made things worse between them." He paused, and gazed out of the doorway. It was very quiet, except for Leonard sitting on the wall outside, snapping at locusts when they bounced too near his face.

"What *did* he do?" I asked at last.

"Well, having co-opted Smenkhkare on to the throne, he sent him and Meritaten back to Thebes to hold out something like an olive branch there."

"Are there any portraits of him or her?" I asked. Tommy dived at the bookcase, and came back with a book in German on the religion and art of Amarna. He flipped over the pages until he found what he wanted. Then he slid the book across the table. It was open at a picture of a square stone plaque, on which two figures were carved in relief. A young man in a flowing pleated kilt, the royal symbol on his forehead, a deep collar-necklace across his breast, was leaning back on a staff held in a delicate right hand. One knee bent, so that the sandalled foot rested nonchalantly on the toes. The whole attitude lackadaisical, unvirile, almost as if the thin body were already in the grip of some hidden, slow-moving disease. A long, thin neck and jutting chin, sunken chest and rather nerveless hands.

In contrast the little royal girl facing him looked twice the man. She had the long narrow head of all Akhenaten's daughters, and the long thin neck, but she held them upright; she was well-knit, the small face alert. She was holding out flowers towards her willowy companion.

"Probably Smenkhkare and Meritaten," Tommy said.

"He reminds me very much of Akhenaten," I said, "and she of Nefertiti. Do you think that one can really count on that as a *real* likeness?"

"Almost certainly a well-drawn family likeness," he said. "The whole idea of the art of the period was to reproduce the exact thing you saw. The artists must have had instructions from Akhenaten himself—and the men of the family probably *did* have some bodily failing which really gave them that look. All the princesses have that long, curious head, but yet they and Nefertiti look much more alive than their husbands and brothers. As if they'd suffered a bit, but much less, from the effects of so much inbreeding."

"When Smenkhkare went to Thebes," said Ralph, "what happened to the old folks at home?" He had just drawn a charming chariot at Hatiay's porch, with little prancing horses wearing plumes on their heads.

"That's where evidence based on statistics comes in," said Tommy. "Like the proportion of Royal names you find in various spots. In the few places that have been dug right up here, the latest built part of the site—including this house, when it was being restored as the Expedition House—nearly all the inscribed objects had the names of Nefertiti; but also a fair proportion with the names of Tutankhaten and his wife Ankhsenpaaten."

"None of Akhenaten?"

"Hardly one," Tommy answered. "The deduction's obvious."

John had come in from the dark-room, and having subsided into a chair with a mug of beer, was listening.

"'But now they are der-rifted *er*-part,'" he murmured, from his extensive Victorian music-hall repertoire.

"They actually parted company?" asked Hilary.

"Yes," John said. "Almost at the end of his reign. She may have left him on her own initiative, or she may have been banished. More likely banished, because in the south of the site her name is chipped away wherever it occurred and Meritaten's substituted. But somehow she managed to bring

Tutankhaten with her up here, and of course all the supporters she could muster."

"Yes, now, what about defacements?" Ralph asked. "Would they have gone as far as to deface *his* name up here, as extreme Atenists? Hatiay's lintel, for instance, where Akhenaten's name was the only thing chipped away? It looks there as if *he* but not the cult was unpopular."

"I wanted to ask that, too," I said.

"None of the defacement of *his* name could possibly have been done while Akhenaten was alive, even at this end of the site," said Tommy, and John nodded. "And in any case Hatiay lived much too near the Main City, and held an important position. Up here they seem to give evidence of the rift in the negative sort of way of not reproducing Akhenaten's name on rings or scarabs any more."

"And whatever her private feelings, Nefertiti would still have given him the outward honour due to Pharaoh," John added. "I suppose it's possible that an official like Hatiay might have had the name taken out from the lintel himself, after Akhenaten's death—which wasn't long after the quarrel—when he saw the way things were going. For all anybody knew Nefertiti would live on for many years, keeping her young Pharaoh-brother true to the Aten. A man in Hatiay's position—if he intended to keep it—needed to be on the right side. *His* line would be 'Down with the traitor to Atenism', and in his case, being a warm man and probably a bit of a cynic, this attitude, as well as making for safety, would have the added charm of disfiguring his nice new lintel as little as possible. . . .

"But of course things didn't work out that way, although when Tutankhaten succeeded as Pharaoh through *his* marriage to a daughter of Akhenaten, he was only about 10, and Nefertiti still had a firm hold on things. But it was nearly the end. Smenkhkare, still at Thebes, had died somewhere about this time, and not long after, Nefertiti herself.

"It was the end not only of the leading figures in the whole affair, but of Atenism itself. But the wholesale violence against the late Pharaoh and his heresy didn't break out until several years later. Certainly not until after Tutankhaten's death at Thebes (which happened when he was only 18, and known, of course, as Tutankhamun), and everything settling back safely to the old ways. For after all he'd been mixed up in it all as a child, and even the most violent reactionaries would have gone carefully in dishonouring people so close to the reigning Pharaoh. But it can't have been long after Tutankhamun's death that they began wiping out every vestige of Akhenaten 'that criminal of Akhetaten'—just in case, I suppose, a spark might flare again, somewhere, some day. Then everything went, his names and portraits, Nefertiti's as well, and the painted and carved symbols of Aten worship."

I knew that Nefertiti's death was also the death-blow to Akhenaten's City. It couldn't have been difficult for the Theban priests and high officials to persuade a young pleasure-loving boy to alter the form of his name, and exchange the seclusion of Akhetaten for the glitter and pomp of the ancient capital.

No one knew where Nefertiti's remains were laid, or indeed if any honour was paid her in death. But now I knew this—that Nefertiti had lived close to this old house where we now sat talking about her; had passed the remaining few bitter years of her life, in the place that she made the last defiant stronghold of Atenism.

Our house, quite close to her northern dwelling that she named 'Castle of the Aten', was very large in comparison to many of the other private houses; perhaps it had belonged to one of her friends, or to a Minister of the new young Pharaoh.

Nefertiti must have known this house. It's not too fantastic to think that sometimes, long ago, people sitting as we were now, in this very room, may have heard the murmur of servants' voices out beyond the Central Room, speaking the lovely name as she drew near: "Nefertiti. It is Nefertiti. The Beautiful Lady comes!" And in a moment she may have passed through this doorway, trodden this floor, and perhaps sat talking to her host with a small sandalled foot resting on this column base by my chair.

A little stooping now, ageing before her time, eyes shadowed with sorrow, the lid drooping rather more noticeably perhaps than it used to do over the impaired eye; the sweet mouth thinner and sharper than in the golden days when she was Akhenaten's 'Great of Favour, Mistress of Happiness, at hearing whose Voice one rejoices, soothing the heart of the King at home, Great and Beloved Wife of the King'. But still proud, still single-minded, very royal.

I missed the talk for a few minutes; for a little, the lamplit room seemed to be dominated by the long dead queen. I knew how dangerous fantasy could be to truth when it was allowed to roam unchecked over the meagre facts of the ancient past; and yet how, sometimes, unconnected cold facts had been fired into a single truth by a sudden brilliant spark of imagination leaping the gap. And with Nefertiti and her family it was, somehow, impossible to remain detached, to hear the bare facts of the lives of those few strange people without finding that they were growing alive. It was so, even with the shadow-king, the shadow-brother, Smenkhkare.

Nor was there much need of subjective fantasy or imagination to make their story more vivid. You learned about them, that was enough; their humanity, hopes, disillusionments, griefs seemed to grow up around them as you listened, until they stood away from the flat impersonal frieze of ancient history, freestanding figures in the round. Of course, this mysterious feeling, this sense of inner comprehension, was partly stimulated by the marvellous character studies left to us in their portraits, painted and modelled and carved in the natural style of the period. I saw that. But only partly, because I do believe that without any portraits at all, something of the strange magic of the Royal people at Amarna would still have drifted down to us through the centuries on the facts alone.

How alike in face and bearing they were, as we watched them emerge from the shadows, and move across the bright faraway stage, to play out the short drama. All with that fine-drawn hollow beneath the high cheekbones; the long sweep of jawbone down to the rounded stubborn chin; the heavy-lidded eyes sunk in large sockets. Even beneath the youthful roundness of Tutankhamun's face, and of his little wife, you can still see the same modelling which would probably have emerged gauntly in the middle-age which neither reached.

They were still talking about the reaction of hatred against Akhenaten.

"You see it, of course, in the tombs as much as anywhere else," John was saying. "Defacement of the king's portrait and inscriptions. And of course, they hacked to pieces the sarco-phagus in his own tomb."

I asked him if any trace at all had ever been found of Nefertiti's burial place.

"No," he said. "Of course there are stories—about as wonderful as they are unreliable—about people at the end of last century seeing a golden coffin carried down from the high desert. But nothing of hers was found in Akhenaten's tomb. It's not even entirely certain that *he* was ever buried in it. But when the tomb was excavated—in the 'eighties—a man's body *was* seen there—a body that had been burned some years after it had been mummified. I think we ought to take a day looking at some of the tombs again, and especially his. I've an idea the Royal Tomb ought to be re-excavated—we *might* come across some fresh clues on the whole question. Anyway it would be a good idea to look round again. Hilda and I went up last year—

and you must all see it. Tomorrow is pay-day. Let's start early the day after, and see as many of the tombs as we can."

The workmen had the day off after pay-day, so that on one day a week there was no digging; usually we used the precious hours catching up on our different jobs. But as it was also the only chance in the week for seeing the rest of the site beyond the actual excavations in progress, the only thing to do was to make what expeditions we could on that day, and fit the leftovers of work into the odd corners of the days ahead.

It was late. Hilary's lizard was asleep on his cuff with a beatific smile, tiny hands and feet spread motionless under the warm beam of lamplight. Tommy put *Religion und Kunst in Amarna* back on the shelf, beamed when I thanked him for expounding, and slipped off to the little room where he copied out and translated the inscriptions, and fragments of inscriptions, which were turning up now every day on clay sealings of wine-jars and meat-jars and ostraca.

I gathered up the day's registered finds and took them through into the antiquity room, sorting them into their groups by the light of an electric torch. A tray of faience rings of many colours, some fragmentary but some unbroken, gleamed red and green and blue and yellow as I added the new pale-blue one with Smenkhkare's name. Here in the darkness lay the small tangible remains of the city, unrelated in themselves, but slowly forming a mass of evidence for those whose skill could conjure out of them their mute story. The shelf-spaces were filling up. So too, perhaps, was my ignorance a bit; for just so was I receiving a store of new facts every day, which were spreading along the empty spaces in my head.

If you stood outside the house and looked towards the dig you could see the line of cliffs slanting away on your left in a south-easterly direction for about three miles, then changing direction southward, and then, as they grew lower and greyer and fainter in the distance, curving round again towards the Nile. Just where the direction changed—three miles away—you could make out a break in the rampart, a shadowy cleft; and it was towards this point that we set out very early two days later.

The opening in the line of cliffs was the entrance to a great dry wadi, a valley winding away from the plain of the city into the heart of the high desert. It took us more than an hour to reach, for it was difficult going over the loose sand and pebbles of the plain. As we approached the cliffs we could see, cut into them, here and there, the narrow dark entrances of the tombs of the nobles and high officials. I knew that there were others to the south, beyond the cleft we were making for; and that none of them was ever used—many were still unfinished when the brief life of the city ended.

At last we were mounting a little in the foothills, and before we entered the sombre valley, I turned round and looked back at the familiar scene. Behind me lay the valley, dark and chilly, still untouched by the morning sun. Far away, opposite this point, the ruins and dump heaps of the Main City showed up very small and clear against the distant palms. We were high enough to see the stretch of river opposite the north headland, gleaming blue above the tops of the palms. Two pinpricks of dazzling white showed where a couple of sailing barges were rounding the point. There it all lay, already warm in the sun, bright, familiar, charming. It looked quite wonderful to me, for secretly the prospect of a day spent in walking between steep hills, intermittently popping in and out of tombs, filled me with melancholy. I've never had much use for vertical scenery at the best of times, but when in addition it is pitted with dark entrances which lead into sloping, crumbling, twisting passages, aversion becomes something like horror. My idea of really good scenery is the Norfolk Broads—where the sky is never hidden, and the tallest peak you are likely to encounter is the sweet line of a sail moving beyond the reeds.

But at least things were better than the day when, with chattering teeth, I shrinkingly followed-my-leader into the Great Pyramid. It's wonderful how curiosity can outweigh reluctance; and by now, growing interest and growing knowledge, each chasing each other round in a rising spiral, had made me very curious indeed to see Akhenaten's burial place. And above and beyond that, nervousness couldn't survive easily when one's companions were no longer polite strangers, but gay and trusted friends. It was all being such fun—so good a life. By now we had settled firmly into a chunky recognizable pattern as a team, uncertainties gone, knowing the best way to get the work done, and how to dovetail our particular job most smoothly into all the others. During the process we had learned a lot about each other—very quickly, as small isolated groups of people usually do—and most of what we learned we liked, so that we laughed a lot, and so far, petty irritations which are bound sometimes to ruffle the surface of camp life, had flattened out again harmlessly in such a kindly set-fair atmosphere.

We marched into the Royal Wadi, for so it is still called. Looking back after a minute or two, I saw that already the view of the open plain was cut off. The valley had changed direction a little, and a spur of rock had slid in behind us, across the way we had come, like an arm barring the way back to the old familiar places.

It was like landing on the darkened side of the moon. We were in a new world. The valley was wide, sweeping up on either side into very steep cliffs, the faces streaked and cracked in vast horizontal striation. There was not a sign of moisture or vegetation. The silence was complete. The floor of the valley was strewn with great boulders which had smashed down from the heights through the ages, crumbling into pebbles and dust. High up on the left side the cliffs gleamed in the sun, and as we picked our way along the ancient shadowed pathway, the light came slowly lower until it was travelling across the floor of the valley towards us.

Then it hit us—the force of the sun beating into that sterile place, and trapped there. In a few minutes we were soaked in perspiration. The rocks on our left and the ground beneath us began to throw off a quivering haze of hot air. We moved further over to the right to keep in the swiftly diminishing shade. But soon we were being forced too high up the slopes of this flank for easy foothold. If we were to keep in the shade we must scramble along over steep loose scree most of the time. The alternative was the path along the valley bottom, now full in the sun, as it wound between the boulders. This we took —at least we could move quickly towards our goal that way. I found myself for once dwelling favourably on the whole idea of tombs—at that moment I could have done with a nice cool tomb to sit in—preferably with a very long passage leading right into the heart of the mountain, as far away from the sun as possible.

This went on for about three miles. Then the scene altered; the valley narrowed sharply and went twisting on its eastward way; but to left and right smaller ravines opened up. John and Hilda and Tommy were ahead, and we saw them stop. John signalled to us with his stick that they were going off to the left; we waved flabbily back, and they disappeared round the corner. We pressed on, Hilary and I by now speechless; with Ralph tagging behind us and occasionally bleating: "Carry me, Mummy!"

We rounded the corner and saw a much narrower valley winding off to the north-east, and rising as it went. The sun was full on our backs now; but a small breeze was coming down the valley, welcoming us along. Perhaps it had travelled all the way across the high plateau of the desert from the Gulf of Suez. Hilary swore he could smell salt in it. We were nearly there. We could see the others, far ahead, pause at the foot of a scree to the left of the ravine. Then they began picking their way slowly up it. When we came up, they were sitting in the shade on a small plateau about fifteen feet above the valley floor, with their backs against the cliff face. And in that cliff face beside them loomed a high, dark opening framed in ancient masonry. And a melancholy voice seemed to echo round that sun-drenched desolate place: "My sepulchre, which is in the Eastern Mountain."

We moved into the entrance and stood for a few moments blinded in the dark, although for the first few yards a good deal of light penetrated into the tomb, reflected from the glare on the opposite side of the narrow valley. The entrance sloped downwards, and almost at once we came to a flight of straight steps, with a path about a yard wide left uncut and smooth in the centre, which had been used for sliding the great sarcophagus down. We must be down to ground level by now, I thought. Ahead a long passage, sloping downwards. We clicked on electric torches, for by now the daylight was filtering away. At the end of the passage we came to another flight of steps, shorter but steeper, with the same smooth slope left in the centre. Down we went. Now we must be well below ground level and far into the depths of the hillside. On we went into a small room with a very rough crumbly floor.

"This is really a deep shaft," said John, "cut in front of the tomb chamber, as an extra guard against robbery. But it was filled up after the tomb was excavated. We ought to clear it again, I think, and go through the filling, soon." I crossed it gingerly, hoping very much that we wouldn't go through the filling even sooner.

Beyond this, the passage widened suddenly into a very large room. This was the main chamber. Empty, crumbling, shabby. There were a few very damaged murals on the left-hand wall. John said that because the rock was poor in quality the walls had been plastered, and the decorations cut in that, which was why they had suffered so much. But we could make out the figures of Akhenaten and Nefertiti and the princesses, adoring the sun disk with its benign rays, each ray ending in a hand held out in blessing. One great pillar, strengthening the roof of the chamber, remained. We moved about very quietly in that strange place. Later on, of course, I saw the famous tombs at Thebes, the brilliantly-coloured reliefs cut in the fine hard rock, as glowing and clear-cut today as ever they were; the sharp cornered passages; the professional guides; the electric light; the sun-glassed tourists moving in and out—but yet of them all, I only remember vividly this dark crumbling tomb of Akhenaten, which only the barest handful of people have entered since the day when the sweating workmen brought the sarcophagus to rest there. I remember it because this lonely tomb was so poignantly in keeping with the whole of Akhenaten's story; its very look of neglect suggested failure. Just as he had stood apart in life, unlike his fellows in body and mind, his hand against tradition, but broken by it in the end, so in death he lay alone, far from his own people; in death too, still hounded by tradition, his body broken and burned by the zealots from Thebes.

As we turned away from the main chamber, I thought of those workmen waiting for the few mourners to move away up into the sunlight so that they could seal the inner door; then slowly mounting the steps as we were now doing, but carrying up the gear they had used, the ropes and rollers and levers; and then beginning the big work of securing the outer entrance. And finally, as evening fell, the work completed, the puzzled voices growing fainter as their footsteps faded away down the valley. Utter silence now. Behind them, deep in the heart of the 'Eastern Mountain', swathed in the chilly wrappings of oblivion, the still figure, austere, uncherished and alone.

Perhaps the workmen were saying in subdued voices, What

112

would happen now? Would the younger Pharaoh come back from Thebes? They *do* say he's on the way out himself. Well if that's so, that might mean the little lad up here (Prosperity to him!)—and *that* would mean Herself behind the throne once more—queer that it's safe to be talking of Her again. . . .

At the top of the inner flight of stairs a dark opening pierced the wall on the left—for there was one other burial in the tomb. In the happy years of unity one great shadow had fallen over the Royal family. The second daughter, the Princess Maketaten, died. Now we were entering her burial chambers. No trace of the sarcophagus, where it had probably stood in the innermost of the three rooms; but the decorated walls themselves told the universal simple tale of family bereavement and pain. Here stand her parents lamenting, and the usual trail of six little girls is now five, the baby held by a nurse. The funeral rites are shown at different stages, the parents standing by the small bier, then the mummy displayed upright beneath a canopy, and in another scene lying below it. These murals, too, were crumbling and fragmentary, eloquent of that distant grief which somehow lingered in the musty air.

We climbed back at last to the daylight; the sky above the towering cliffs seemed wonderfully blue at that moment; and the rays of the sun disk beat down gratefully on our chilled hearts and bodies.

I don't know what the others were thinking as we set out down the valley again after we had rested and eaten, towards the open plain and the tombs of the nobles. But none of us talked very much. Perhaps they too felt as if they were moving in the small company of shadowy mourners, who must have trodden the same path all those years ago. The sunbaked valley, twisting and turning, must have looked just the same to them.

In the middle of the afternoon we rounded the last spur, and came again into the world we knew; only the light had changed since the morning. Away across the plain, the city now lay in shadow. And in the same way, my feeling about it would never be quite the same again. The light had changed; I would no longer be able to see it detachedly, a remote observer, knowing its story and yet quite uninvolved emotionally. I would feel the shadow over it, feel in my heart the failure underlying the great endeavour; for now, as I walked about its sunny streets and houses, helping to salvage one charming object after another, I would be aware of the end of it all; aware of a dark cleft parting the once unbroken ramparts, and of a harsh and comfortless path leading away inevitably to a rough, unhallowed tomb.

Chapter Ten

THE weather was changing. It was January; still too early for the regular khamsin—we should be gone by the time that was due in early March—but every now and then a dry hot wind blew from the south, carrying with it clouds of dust and sand which dimmed the sun and discoloured the sky and made things uncomfortable. The gritty sand was everywhere—drying the skin, and soiling your fingers as you touched tables and chairs and books. It got through the tightly closed office window, and drifted down the paper in the typewriter; and when I tried to blow it off, the grains which had landed on the typed words, still slightly wet from the ink on the ribbon, stuck there, so that I found myself producing a sort of pale yellow raised gesso work—highly picturesque and intriguing, if you happened to be in the mood to find it so.

I was not. I'd been doing sums that morning, and it seemed to me that including our next and last draft from London, we should only have the money to carry on the dig for a month longer at best, instead of the six or seven or even eight weeks that John was hoping for before the khamsin made conditions impracticable to go on; and he wouldn't like it when he heard the news, and saw the figures in black and white.

Lack of money was the bogy looming behind every small expedition of this kind. We had to rely on a few large donations from private sources, and for the rest on anything else the Society itself could squeeze out. An unhealthy situation; for if the few big patrons dropped out, we were done.

The only way to plan a long-term campaign comprising several seasons' work would be if an assured income were to come from a great many people giving smallish donations quite steadily. But it was hardly likely that a large proportion of the British public would ever be intrigued enough about the non-spectacular side of archaeology to the extent of parting with its pennies in such a cause. There was no doubt about the pull that a spectacular find could produce, in the way first of interest, and then money. Tutankhamun's tomb had proved that; it was only natural. Yet even in that phenomenal case the interest of the mass of people waned after a few years, and with it their donations, so that season-planning on a grand scale was out of the question.

On the scientific side this season was perfectly satisfactory; the work went steadily and efficiently on, properly recorded and planned and reported; and there were many interesting finds and a few first-class ones. But you could see that there was nothing that would exactly have the British public in a fighting mass on the doorstep of our Society, waving cheque books and purses, frantic to keep us in the field at all costs.

Uncertainty also made the winding-up of any season very difficult; if he didn't know whether he was coming back in the autumn or not, a Director had a great problem—whether it was profitable to use his precious time and men digging every tiny house (although any of them, however unlikely looking, *might* produce something important); or whether he ought to range rapidly over a larger area, selecting important-looking houses which he could not be sure of ever having a chance to dig again. I knew that this hit-and-miss method would go against the grain with John.

I knew, too, that he was clinging to his original plan of finishing off the whole of the North Suburb this season; and that the work was almost too much for our small staff. Hilary and Ralph were surveying all day, and drawing up the plans late into the night; and to help them John and Tommy were sharing between them most of the early overseeing of the dig, which meant getting up every other day at 5.30, with something like 16 hours' working-day ahead. The strain was beginning to show. Ralph had not been looking well for some days.

Hilda and I were trying to produce between us complete painted copies, in diagram form, of the patterns found on some painted beams which had fallen with the ceiling in one house. If there had been plenty of time to settle to it, it would have been fun; but there was a nightmarish feeling of pressure behind it all, the consciousness of other jobs waiting to be done and steadily piling up.

A step in the courtyard interrupted my joyless meditations, and Ralph came into the office. He tried unsuccessfully for a moment to open the medicine cupboard door, and then sat down on a chair.

"It's locked," I said. "What's the matter?" He was staring at me out of a grey, dust-streaked face.

"Thought I'd better come up to the house and die here," he said wearily. "I do feel so bad."

I found a thermometer, and had that uncomfortable shock when you see the black line way up in the red beyond where it ought to be.

"It *is* a bit above normal," I said guardedly. "You'd better go and lie down."

"Come on, show me," he said. "I can tell from your face."

I handed the thermometer over. He twiddled it about inexpertly for a moment, and then frowned at it. "A hundred and three plus," he murmured. "Thought as much. Well, it's no good trying to work like this. I can hardly see for headache —haven't been able to draw a straight line for the last day or two. I'll go and sit in the living-room—it's cooler there."

"Bed," I said. "Go on. We'll come and see how you are at teatime. Back to the basket for Bertram."

He grinned, got up slowly, and disappeared towards his

117

room. I went and found Hilda. We followed him up and found him shivering and saying he would get up after supper and finish off the plan of T.36.36, which John badly wanted. We told him gently not to be a chump.

"I expect he'll be all right if we keep him quiet for a bit," Hilda said uncertainly, as we walked back from his room, "but John will be frantic. We're slipping behind schedule; he was saying this morning that there really ought to be one more person to take on some of the supervision—and now with one *less* . . ."

She went off to find aspirins and barley-water, asking me to fill a hot-water bottle.

After that I went back to the office. Evening was coming, and the view beyond the window was not cheerful. Peevish gusts fretted and slapped round the house; a hot gritty haze hid the sky, and the grey dusty palms tossed angrily in the wind. I saw John and Hilary and Tommy coming slowly out of the dust cloud. It looked to me as if John were limping slightly. Now what?

In a few moments he came quietly into the office, laid down a camera and his notebooks, and went out again without speaking. I went round to the drawing-office where Hilary was stacking his drawing-board and measuring tapes. "How's Ralph?" he asked.

I told him, and said he wasn't likely to be fit for anything for a few days.

"Well, I can't do more than my own plans," he said desperately; "and John wants to start a new house and estate tomorrow."

"What's the matter with him?" I asked.

He looked surprised. "He *says* he's quite all right now—how on earth did you know?"

"Limping and gloomy," I said. "What happened?"

"He knelt on a big scorpion at midday," he answered,

"when he was examining a wall niche. It obviously hurt him a lot. Then he was very sick, and said he felt better—but I think his knee is still swollen—he didn't want it mentioned."

We went into the living-room for a late tea. John was already having a cup of tea, but not eating anything. I knew that a bad sting from a big scorpion might be serious. It could easily kill a child. He looked rather pale, but quite calm. Hilda had of course found out what had happened, and he had just heard about Ralph. I devoutly hoped that I wouldn't have to break the news about our finances on this wretched evening.

"Don't you think he'll be better by tomorrow?" he asked Hilda anxiously.

"Sorry, John, but you mustn't think of it," she answered. "Even when he's down to normal he won't be fit to go charging round the dig for a day or two after a turn like this; it would probably have been better if he'd given up sooner. You'll simply have to reckon without him for at least three or four days, I should think—and we don't really know what's the matter with him. You ought to take a day off up here yourself, with that knee."

"Can't be done," he said stubbornly. "I shall be all right tomorrow. And if we have to slow down a bit now, we can make it up by staying on a bit longer than we meant—say till eight weeks from now."

I saw it coming.

"I expect we can work it, can't we?" he went on, turning round to me. "From the money point of view, I mean? Is it possible to calculate at this point how things are panning out?"

There was nothing for it.

"I made some calculations today, John," I said. "As near as possible. And I'm afraid the position isn't too good. Since we took on twenty-five more workmen, the weekly labour bill alone is nearly £60, counting the Guftis and the household people. As far as I can see the money will only last another five weeks at the very outside. We'd need at least another £200 to carry on three weeks beyond that."

There was an uncomfortable silence. An unhappy captain makes an unhappy crew. I could see him calculating five weeks in terms of the North Suburb, bad weather and a tiring staff; could see that he was recognizing that it was impossible; could see him absorbing the disappointment into a body still shocked and aching with the scorpion's venom.

"I see," he said at last, quietly. "Well—that's *that*. We must just get as far as we can now, and make quite certain we come out again next winter—and somehow with bigger funds." We watched him climbing painfully out of the depths. "We must think out plans *now* for raising money all through the summer," he went on slowly. "Make the exhibition tremendously attractive to a great many people somehow—and meanwhile"—he smiled rather bitterly—"hope for buried treasure— £200 of it."

Hussein came in with a pile of mail which had just arrived. His eyes were scared as he told us of the great waves on the river, and how wet the felucca boys were after taking nearly an hour to row across the rough water. They hadn't dared raise the sail.

Tommy took Ralph's letters round to him, and came back to say he was asleep.

"I don't believe we could get the little Syrian doctor from Mallawi to come across in this weather," said Hilda. "I *do* hope he won't be any worse tomorrow."

John dealt round the letters; and for some moments there wasn't a sound except the crackling of opened envelopes and unfolding papers, and the wind fussing round the courtyard.

After a minute or two he said, "Here's a funny thing, coming just now." We all looked up. "A letter from a young American asking if he could come and help on the dig for a

THE POST BOY

bit, for his keep—'as digs interest him'. George Somebody, writing from Luxor—tourist, I suppose."

"Sounds like an answer to prayer," said Hilary sleepily.

We talked it over. He might be useless, he might be invaluable. Finally John said that we couldn't really afford to turn down *any* offer of help at this point; and Hilda agreed thankfully, but said what about room-space.

"Would you and Hilary mind doubling up in your room, Tommy?" she asked. They both shook their heads.

"Well, then, would you write and say he can come?" John asked me, handing over the letter. "And the sooner the better —and do make it clear it's no picnic. He'll get a shock if he's expecting something like the American expedition house **at**

Luxor. What couldn't we do with a fraction of the money they spend there on Swiss chefs and bathrooms."

I took the letter off into the office with the rest of the business mail, and drafted an answer before supper. I thought, as I was doing it, that John would probably never have taken the risk of admitting a total stranger into our small, remote circle in normal times. The chance of such a newcomer not fitting in was too great. Anyone who has lived in a small withdrawn community for months on end knows the psychological storms that can blow up even among good mixers when nerves are getting edgy—and how such storms if protracted can endanger an entire expedition. But the need for extra help, and the coincidence of the letter coming exactly when it did, tipped the balance in the stranger's favour. Omens and auguries seemed more significant at Amarna than in England. And if by a miracle he turned out to be phenomenally adaptable, intelligent and hardworking, all without setting the payroll back by so much as a piastre, he might even be the solution to the problem of the completion of the North Suburb.

At this point I took a look at the rather flabby handwriting again; and without being a handwriting expert, felt exceedingly doubtful that any such happy outcome was ahead of us.

The next few days were not good. John was driving himself grimly; and although Ralph's fever subsided steadily, it was a slow process. The dust still swirled in the air, and more and more of the workmen came up to the house each evening with bloodshot eyes and dry coughs after the long hours out in the open. In this sort of weather they would normally have kept close under the trees, or near the river, head shawls swathed thick over foreheads and noses and mouths, away from the fly-ridden dust.

Then came a day when the wind dropped to a light breeze, the dust settled, the sky changed slowly from its ugly haze to clear pearl and then palest blue; and we heard that our new boy would be at the station early that afternoon. The boat was sent off in the morning, and Hilda and I went down to the river before tea, and watched the tiny felucca under its odd-shaped gleaming sail—much too big for it, it always looked—growing larger as it bobbed up and down towards us on the still lively water.

As it drew nearer, we could see expensive-looking suitcases piled everywhere. In the middle of it all rose the dome of a pale brown sun-helmet. The boys brought the felucca neatly alongside, and stretched their hands out over the cases towards the dome. It rose up slowly and revealed a round and pallid face followed by a beautiful pale tussore suit, the whole effect that of a lightly toasted marshmallow. It stepped gingerly ashore and came up holding out a plump hand.

The boat-boys were setting ashore his endless trousseau. Alongside our new playmate they looked incredibly fit and alive—even beautiful—with their spare dark skin, like beaten copper, taut over the bone, and muscle rippling just beneath the surface. We had become so used to this look of fine-drawn vigour, that I suppose George started off at an unfair disadvantage.

He was young and quite tall, but pudgy—a pale face; thin, crinkly fair hair already retreating smartly; a small parroty nose above a full mouth; and a weak chin in duplicate. In profile he looked like one of the rather less attractive Roman Emperors.

For a minute or two we all made affable and stilted remarks. Then in single file we started off up the narrow path, which ran between a deep ditch and someone's onion bed, making the sort of depressing conversation you would expect when it is over your shoulder to start with, and you also have a conviction that plump disaster is trailing in the rear. He suggested that a motor-launch would be a good idea when the river was so wide here; said that it was truly wonderful to be

123

in the wilds of Egypt; and that he sure was looking forward to a shower.

Hilda said that we rather liked our old felucca; I said **we** didn't find things particularly wild in these parts; and we **both** said we were afraid he wouldn't be able to have a shower. In the silence that followed, while we concentrated on not falling into the ditch¯ or stepping on the onions, we didn't have to wonder what the others would think.

Supper was a subdued affair: I think we did our best; but English people *are* bad at opening their citadel to a stranger, even when he is obviously a kindred spirit. They peer at him through the arrow-slits and battlements for days and days, warily trying to sum up the character and intentions of the stranger at the gate. If he happens to be English himself, or if not that, then used to the ways of the tribe, he recognizes the manœuvre, and remains patiently parked on the sward beyond the moat until somebody lets him in. But if the stranger is a young American, he must be genuinely amazed at the time it takes to lower the drawbridge.

George tried to rush it, which was a fatal beginning. He said he felt sure we all had nicknames, and would like to know them; he was always called 'Doc' back home, on account he was so interested in dosing himself and his friends. His principal activities seemed to be conjuring, and experimenting with hypodermic needles.

John gazed at his plate and said that neither accomplishment would be much in demand at Amarna, and did he know any Arabic? It appeared not, as he had only reached Cairo a fortnight ago, after several weeks in Europe, and had spent a week with the American Expedition in Luxor. He spoke lyrically of the refrigerators there, the badminton court, and the library with its parquet flooring.

"Because we do want your help down at the dig, as well as on odd jobs up here," John went on, breaking in on the paean.

"We're short-handed and have a great deal to get through in the next few weeks. When you come down tomorrow morning, I'll show you round. You'll have to try and learn enough to know what the Reis in charge is trying to tell you—I'll give you a list of the most used words and phrases. But even if you understand him, you mustn't make *any* decision on your own without reporting first to one of us."

The words came out quietly and pleasantly—but it looked as if George had realized then for the very first time that in offering to come and work here he had been taken quite seriously. Realized too for the first time that John, in spite of his youthful and casual manner, was boss—that he had given him an order, and would go on doing so for as long as he elected to stay here and help consume our good—if unrefrigerated—food.

He shot John a curious look of surprised and rather amused respect—with a touch of the sulks thrown in. The amusement was probably meant to be a trifle patronizing, by way of saving his face in his own esteem.

"Sure I'll come down tomorrow morning," he said. "I never could do languages—but I'll try. I've read up on this place, though. Didn't Toot'nkhamen live right here? And didn't they find that head of Nefertiti here?"

"Sure they did," Ralph murmured, looking rather groggy and glum after his first day up. "I expect you're hoping to fall over gold coffins at every turn."

George laughed. "I'm not that much of a sucker," he said affably; and I suddenly felt we were all being rather tediously British. We were ganging up on him. But his next words made me gang harder than ever. "But maybe you'll find something sensational while I'm here—I could use it. I've an arrangement with a paper back home to cable them any noos they would call sensational."

John sat up. He told George in no uncertain terms that a London paper had first call on all our news, and that to send news anywhere else first would be a breach of that agreement. "You do understand that, don't you?"

"Sure I do—it's just too bad, that's all."

"I'm sorry, but there it is—you're not a journalist by profession, are you?"

"No, indeed," he answered. "I haven't rightly settled on a profession yet since I left Princeton. My Dad sent me on this trip hoping I'd have made up my mind by the time I got back. But I guess I haven't given it a lot of thought; but I've certainly had a good time." He giggled reminiscently, and looking at his sleek, blasé visage, it wasn't difficult to imagine the kind of adventures that Dad back home had been financing.

We gathered that Dad had never stopped working in his life, but wanted Sonny to have the good time he'd never had at that age. I felt sorry for Dad. He sounded like Kipling's ship-and-railroad millionaire whose small spoilt son had his body and soul saved alive by falling overboard from a liner and being picked up by a fishing schooner off the Banks. Only George hadn't had the luck to fall overboard anything in time. He was a soft playboy from a padded world; and what seemed natural and good to us in a camp life—campbeds, oil lamps, tin baths on the floor and all the rest of it—must have seemed really shockingly primitive and unbearable to him. Yet to some of the pioneer archaeologists of the century before, whose only furniture and shelter were sometimes a few packing cases inside a rock tomb, and only nourishment for weeks on end bread and sardines and coffee, our standard of camp living would have seemed shockingly luxurious.

We'd all heard of this type of young American—mostly through fiction—and it was just bad luck that by chance the first one that most of us ever came across in real life happened to match a preconceived idea. So for a time after this I, at any rate, in my youthful, smug and insular way, made the big mistake of thinking that George really was typical of the great mass of transatlantic young men. Luckily for me it wasn't long before I worked with many other Americans, who cured me from making snap judgements based on a single example. And although I still think they can be practically morbid in their concentration on hygiene and personal comfort—and although I'm quite sure they consider my standard of living not far removed from that of the Dark Ages—it hasn't prevented the growth of deep and lifelong friendships.

Meanwhile we were young and ruthless; without the time or the inclination to let George down gently.

The next day he hadn't appeared by the time breakfast was over; but just as I was getting ready to go down to the dig and begin a copy of a painted wall fragment which had been reported, Hussein came in with a jug of fresh coffee and suppressed hysterics.

George followed, all set for a day on a dig.

Starting at the top, there was the brown sun-helmet. Then a long white neck, that would have left Annie Laurie standing. Then a little-boy jersey in pale blue, with a round neckline, and tiny short sleeves. Following on down, incredibly brief, dazzlingly white shorts; then an astonishing length of thin white leg ending in tiny pale blue ankle-socks, and white buckled sneakers. He carried a fly-whisk, studded with pale blue beadwork.

I'm afraid I murmured "Hooray for Captain Spalding!" having encountered the famous African explorer in the person of Groucho Marx, complete with sun-hat, cigar, raven moustache and glasses, only a few months before.

He obviously recognized the quotation, and grinned rather sheepishly. "Anything wrong with my turnout?"

I thought of Hussein's face; he had very good manners. Then I thought of the hundred or so rough workmen down at the dig, who certainly had not. It never took much to make them laugh. A discreet ankle was as much as you ever saw of an Egyptian's leg, unless he were a boat-boy or fisherman with gowns looped up into their belts. I felt sure that George's little shorts and long straggling legs would cause a riot, and stop the show; for the dig's sake as well as his, I must somehow get him into long trousers before he left the house.

The argument that although it was all right by us the workmen would either be shocked or laugh their heads off, left him unmoved. He didn't mind what a bunch of primitive darkies thought. The argument that the dig was a very dusty, rough place when the work was in full swing, and that his dazzling whites would be black in no time, and his soft shoes in ribbons, had rather more weight; but what shifted him finally into long khaki pants was my sad prediction that with so much of him exposed to the teeth and claws and talons of every passing sandfly, he would almost certainly be in a high fever by evening. This was an inspiration, and not entirely a whopper—we'd all had a touch of sandfly fever at the beginning of the season—and anyway it did the trick. He looked very solemn and said he didn't have an anti-sandfly serum in his medical outfit. I looked very solemn back at him, and said, well then, the more of him that was covered up the better; and half an hour later we set out decorously together, George in the aforesaid khaki trousers, with the addition of a cowboy neckerchief tied jauntily under one ear, and smelling to Heaven of Midgescare.

I really believe that compared to his normal life, what he did at Amarna was to him real hard work. But being so used to it ourselves, his own efforts didn't strike us in the same way. Even the mile walk to and from the dig every day nearly killed him at first.

"Never walked further than two blocks at home," he confided to us one warm evening, subsiding in a heap on the outer wall. "Just jumped in my auto—say, why don't you have an auto here? Look at the time and energy you'd save." John, who loathed cars, and only tolerated them as necessary evils that happened in the life across the river, and would have considered it downright sacrilege to have one at Amarna, said nothing; but he looked rather like Edward III being told that he ought to have this wonderful new cannon that everybody was talking about, at his next battle. He had become rather more noticeably medieval since George's arrival.

The days went on, and it began to dawn on George that for the most part, digging an ancient site consisted of a rather monotonous routine which needed all the unflagging meticulous conscientious patience of a good black-coated worker, combined with the physical fitness of a trained athlete. And although he struggled along with the assignments he was given, he stayed outside it all, in a mood of almost amused contempt, simply because he hadn't a clue really as to what it was all about. He would have taken a showy find very seriously indeed. The shelves in the antiquity room, crowded by now, left him fairly cold, as he hadn't the knowledge to see the significance of any of the small objects. Nobody blamed him for not knowing anything; but he never seemed to think it worth his while to begin to find out. Inevitably he began to get horribly bored. No loot, no fun. Instead of impressing his young friends back home with tales of supervising the excavation of ancient treasure, he would have to make up for it by giving sidesplitting accounts of life among the barbarous British. I felt sure he would do it rather well, as he was a bit of a comedian when he could forget for a few minutes the rigours of his Spartan existence.

It seemed he hardly could wait, for after about three weeks came an alleged summons in the mail from the Old Man. For one who put up such an air of worldly wisdom, he could be touchingly transparent. We had gradually come to feel sure, from one or two things he had let out, that one reason for his staying the course even as long as he did, was that he had overrun the constable properly, was scared of telling Dad, and that he was hanging on where he had no expenses until rescue, in the shape of another of Dad's hard-earned drafts, landed safely in a Cairo Bank. Hilary told us later that he let on to him just before he left, that it was indeed news of this happy event, and no summons, which had decided him to let go his tenuous hold on his first real job of work.

Anyway he asked John, rather uncomfortably, if he thought perhaps he could manage without him for the rest of the season; and John, making up for all the refrigerators that Amarna hadn't got, replied that he thought perhaps he could.

No loot, no fun. Poor old George. For the very day he was to leave, it happened.

Chapter Eleven

IT was another uncomfortable blowy day of grit and haze. I had just finished copying a painted wall fragment, a stretch of about two feet showing a bird flying against a bright yellow background. The eye still gleamed soft and bright and dewy, the feathers on the grey neck and outstretched wings were dappled green and purple. It glowed with an iridescent sheen out of the dusty rubble of the low ruined wall. John wanted to get the original away from the wall, if possible, and taken up to the house. So now Hilda and I were busy on the tricky business of detaching the plaster on which the painting had been done—a skin only a fraction of an inch thick—from the wall behind it. Actually what we did was to take the wall away from the plaster, following a technique worked out by Petrie nearly fifty years earlier.

First of all we sprayed the front of the painting with a solution of celluloid in amyl acetate—which is much the same as nail varnish—putting a thin, transparent but strengthening coat over the terribly fragile painted surface. Then, working from behind the low wall, we loosened the mud bricks and cut them away bit by bit. A young Gufti, sitting by us, stirred a bowl of plaster of Paris, keeping it from setting before it was needed. As the tiny crevices developed between bricks and painting, we dripped in spoonfuls of plaster, until at last the painting was backed by a new white wall, about an inch thick. After that there would be a long wait while the plaster hardened properly, before the final process of moving the whole fragment could begin.

We were waiting for the plaster to set, when we heard Old Umbarak's whistle. As it was in the middle of the afternoon, this was odd. We looked across the North Suburb and saw a crowd of workmen gathered in a small house which was being dug quite close to the cultivation. More and more of the workmen were moving in that direction to see what was going on. Discipline seemed to have slipped completely for a moment. I think Hilda and I both thought 'Accident' in our hearts. It would have been only too easy to break an arm or leg by falling into one of the deeper pits or trenches. Hilda told the boy to guard the painting carefully until we came back, and we moved across to see what had happened.

At the centre of the crowd everyone was staring down at the floor of a humble little room in the small house T.36.63, the walls of which ran nearly up to the green line of spring maize marking the edge of the cultivation. A Gufti and a tourieh man were kneeling in the sand beside a large pot lying on its side, which we were told had been found in the cavity to be seen in the floor. A pottery saucer with a crack across it, which had served as a lid until the Gufti eased it off, lay close by. But it was neither the hole in the floor nor the crock nor the saucer which held our gaze; it was what lay on the dun-coloured sand in front of the dark mouth of the pot—gleaming yellow bars. As the Gufti shook the jar gently and put in a dark hand to ease out more of the contents, another and yet another shining bar slid out, and lay on the growing heap, and winked and shimmered in the sun. Solid gold; and then came a shower of dull white bars and rings and coils—could they be silver?

The whole dig seemed to be there, mostly silent with surprise, but an occasional "Ma'sh'allah!" and "Wah! wah! wah!" burst out. We heard afterwards that when the Gufti in charge had seen the first ingot and recognized it for what it was, he had sent a quiet message over to Old Umbarak to ask John to come, thinking that was better than sending one of the locals. But Old Umbarak, scenting something interesting, had come himself, lost his head in his excitement, and worst of all, blown his whistle. If he had kept calm, it might have been possible to shut the pot again, and have it taken up to the house quietly. As it was, the news was all over the dig in a flash, the amount of gold and silver found in the hoard swelling by several hundredweights every time the news was recounted; and there was no chance now of keeping dark that we had come upon a hoard of gold and silver, quite embarrassingly large even without any fantastic exaggerations. It must have been hidden by a robber of Akhenaten's time; it might even be melted down treasure stolen from the Temple or the Palace.

More ingots and coils of white silver tumbled out. Finally a large gold bar about a foot long, and a thin trickle of grey sand. There was something gleaming in it. The Gufti picked it out and handed it up to John. It was a tiny amulet figure about an inch high, made of silver with a ring at the back to thread on a chain. On the head with its large eyes and beaky nose, was a little round cap of gold. It was as if the gold and silver amulet had been slipped in as a kind of mascot, to guard the hoard made up of the same stuff of which he himself was fashioned, until times were safe for his master to unearth the treasure. But for some reason that time had never come; the man who had filled that crock and covered the mouth with a pottery lid, and buried it all so carefully under the floor of his little house, must have died with his secret intact and untold.

There was a sudden outbreak of chatter and gesticulation as the men went back to work. John saw to the transfer of the find up to the house, with Hilary to escort it and stay with it for the rest of the day; Ralph was up there already, catching up on his plans against time; and George was packing, for he was crossing the river that evening to catch the night train to Cairo. When Hilary and the crock of gold had gone, John came over to the place where Hilda and I were once again concentrating on our charming but agonizingly frail bird. He was worried. The men working on the dig were friendly enough, mostly simple, goodhearted souls; but there were plenty of toughs about, up and down the cultivation, especially among the few malcontents who had lost jobs on the dig for one reason or another.

It was unlikely, but just possible, John thought, that the news of a lot of gold up at the house, might be followed by trouble of some kind; the least being an attempted theft by one or two men, the worst an organized attack. "Not from any of our workmen," he said, stubbornly loyal, "I'm sure of that. But the news will spread far beyond the villages in the cultivation. The silly part is that from the point of view of archaeology it has absolutely no value whatever—except the little amulet, which I think is Hittite. All the rest is just melted down gold and silver."

"Well, it all comes of hoping for buried treasure," said Hilda cheerfully, bandaging a thick layer of cotton wool all over a drawing-board. "You've asked for it."

"Yes, so I did—£200 of it." He laughed. "I suppose Cairo will take it all at the Division—but if they *do* divide it with us, I wonder if we could possibly convert our share into funds for the dig next year—I'd *like* to dig on funds which had actually been left to us by an eighteenth-dynasty robber."

The plaster had set firm. John brought the padded board to the wall, and very carefully held it upright, almost, but not quite, touching the coat of varnish. I held the edges of the plaster while Hilda worked a knife along the lower edge. In a minute or two I could feel that the plaster was only supported by my fingers; it swayed slightly as I moved them. John brought the board a fraction closer; I pressed the plaster very gently forward, and then at a word from Hilda he lowered the board away backwards till it lay on the ground with the painting face downwards on its padded surface. We breathed again. We shouldn't be able to tell if the painting had suffered until we got it off the board again up at the house, but if the plaster and the varnish held, all would probably be well.

The young Gufti set off slowly for the house carrying the board with infinite care.

We gathered our paraphernalia of mixing bowls, knives, the spray, spoons, cotton wool, bandages and all the rest of it, packed them into a large box, and told one of the big basket-boys to bring it up to the house later. John left Tommy in charge of the dig and came up with us.

" Master George will kick himself at missing all this," he said. "He'll probably want to stay on now—but out he goes. I feel rather as if for the past three weeks I'd been taking a jelly-fish for a walk on the end of a piece of rather worn elastic."

"He's lost pounds in the process," I said. "He was beginning to look quite thin and brown."

"I expect it was mainly Dad's fault," said Hilda. "He wasn't such a bad lad really—simply allowed to grow up flabby. Do slow down, John."

"I'm sure it's all a matter of early training," he said, dropping back again to our pace. "I should have been abominably lazy myself if my father hadn't seen to it from the start."

The effort of picturing John being abominably lazy occupied my powers of imagination for the rest of the walk back.

At the house we found Ralph grimly drawing plans, and crossly telling Hilary, every time he saw him pass the open doorway of the drawing-office, not to be melodramatic; for, faithful unto death, Hilary had parked the crock of gold in the antiquity room, and was now moving alertly up and down the courtyard with a drawn revolver. He was enjoying himself no end; and the Abu Bakr family were grouped in the kitchen doorway, suitably impressed—at least they were saying: "Wah! wah! wah!" in turn, which seemed to be the Egyptian equivalent for "Cor'!"

George had gone.

"But the train doesn't get here from Luxor till about 10 p.m.," said John. "When did he go?"

"About half an hour after I got up here," said Hilary. "He was terribly excited about the treasure. First time I'd seen him look as if he wasn't half asleep. He rounded up the felucca boys and off they went. Ralph went down to the river to see him off—I couldn't go, of course, as I was on guard."

"Thought *someone* ought to see the chap off," said Ralph. "He knew he hadn't been much use, all right. I expect he went early to avoid embarrassing good-byes all round."

"Possibly," John said thoughtfully. "I wonder."

Tommy arrived from the dig and said all was calm. Apparently the workmen were laughing their heads off over a wretched man who owned the maize plot next to T.36.63, the House of the Crock of Gold. He had a donkey, which for years he had tethered to a stake driven in to the waste ground a few feet out from his field. It was the point of that stake which had cracked the pottery lid covering the hoard, a foot or so below the ground. And now to find that for years he had daily been standing above untold riches. . . . His remarks, which had clearly entranced the workmen, had been pithy. Tommy's only regret was that for the most part they went well outside his own respectable scope of Arabic.

After supper we looked at the painting. This was done by simply laying a very light drawing-board over the plaster, and then carefully turning the whole sandwich—two boards with the painting between—right way up. After this part of the manœuvre was accomplished, nobody had the nerve to lift the original board off the painting in case the worst had happened.

"Go on, somebody," said John, "watch the pretty birdie."

We lifted off the board nervously, and put it down on the floor. It was all right. In the soft light of the oil lamp the grey and green and purple-flecked feathers still winged across the primrose sky, the soft eye still shone—a little dimmer perhaps under the new surface, but full and round and dark.

"Lovely," said John. "We shall have to have a special case made for shipping it, though. And I think young Sawag deserves some baksheesh; he must have taken a lot of trouble to get that up safely."

He went away to the office to write an article on the last few weeks' work, culminating in the strange find of the day. This would be sent to the London paper, with copies to the Department of Antiquities in Cairo, and the London office. Meanwhile, I settled down to the day's registration, including the hoard, for it was an inflexible rule, and a good one, that everything must be recorded and labelled on the same day that it was found. By now all the others were too hectically busy with the struggle to keep up to date with their own specialist jobs to be able to lend a hand. It took a long time, and as I sleepily tied the last label and entered the last fragment, the gold and silver spread out on the long table seemed to be melting together under the lamplight into a shining, rippling pool. I left the little Hittite amulet to the end, and then took him through to the antiquity room, and gave him a small white cardboard box all to himself, lined with cotton wool.

After three thousand years he was quit of his responsibility; for that night John had the rest of the hoard moved into his own room; and to Hilary's joy, asked whether he might borrow his revolver. All the leg-pulling he had endured on the lines of Intrepid Boy Explorer and so on was forgotten when he realized that the cause of it all—his little gun—was coming into its own at last. He began to explain all its works to John at length. "I don't mean to use it, you know," John said gently. "All I want is something to put off any possible intruder—not that I really think anything is at all likely to happen."

"And there's always Leonard," said Hilary, half proudly, half sadly. "He'd never let anyone through."

Nothing did happen, then or later. Leonard barked like a fiend once, and I suppose Hilary's hopes rose for a moment; but soon the great singing silence of Amarna settled again.

The felucca boys had been told to stay over on the other side of the river that night, after they had taken George to the station, so that they could bring back mail due the next day. Late in the afternoon the following day, while I was finishing typing out the article and reports which John had written the evening before, one of the boys came lightly to the office door, wet through from the choppy water which the little tub of a felucca shipped continually in bad weather, and handed in the pile of mail and a parcel or two. He went off with a flash of white teeth—a cheering sight in the dusty haze; even if the skies rained grit and the waters rose, the Egyptians still beamed at you.

There was a telegram on the top of the pile, addressed to the Director of Excavations. I wondered about it as I extracted my own letters and a parcel of prints from Cairo. I didn't have to wonder long. I could see some of the Guftis coming up from the dig. Soon after John came into the office and saw the mail on his table. He picked up the telegram and frowned at it. Then he tore it open and there was a long sizzling silence.

"Well, I half expected it," he said at last, almost to himself. He handed the paper across. It came from a New York paper via its Cairo office; and was to the effect that it was prepared to splash the story of the hoard of gold, but wished confirmation and a short copyright exclusive article cabled at once.

For a moment it seemed unbelievable magic to me. "From *New York*?" I said. "But we only found the hoard yesterday afternoon. How could they possibly——?"

He looked at me as if I were dotty.

"George, of course," he said. "He didn't lose a second, tearing off like that." He called to Hussein to find one of the felucca boys, and then we went into the living-room and told the others what had happened.

"But he knew about your commitments with London," Hilda said furiously. I think she was angrier with George for landing this new worry on John than for the exploit itself.

"Yes, he did," he answered, in a discouraged sort of voice. "But probably told himself that as he was no longer on the staff, it was all right. Which technically and legally, I suppose, is so. Any free-lance reporter is at liberty to turn in news that he comes across, I imagine. But on moral grounds . . ."

"He obviously thought *he* would be asked for the article," said Hilary. "He was out for all the extra money he could lay hands on, apart from Pop's allowance."

"Yes, of course," said John. "But luckily for us and not so luckily for him, the paper has behaved very correctly, and wired direct to the dig. A nasty shock for Master George; and it's bad luck for the paper, because I shall have to say no article, and tell them to lay off."

He began to draft a cable explaining the situation, that nothing should be published until it had first appeared in London. Then he wrote another one to London, saying that an article was going off by Air Mail at once, and that any leakage of the same news was beyond his control. "Because he may try again elsewhere."

Hussein came in to say that the felucca boy, Mohammed, was in the office, and we went round to see him. Yes, the gentleman had sent young Ali to the station with all his luggage, and had taken himself, Mohammed, to show the way to the Telegraph Office. Yes, the gentleman had stayed in the Telegraph Office a long, long time; then he had gone to the hotel for dinner to wait for the train.

Meanwhile I had got the report and its copies ready for posting, and the two cables printed out. John asked Hilary if he would go across at once and try and get them all sent off before the Post Office shut down for the night. "If you can't, first thing in the morning—you'll have to stay overnight anyway, it's nearly dark now. It's vital to get all this straightened out quickly."

Hilary was ready in five minutes, and loped off towards the cultivation, with the two boys' brown feet slip-slapping after him. They had both crossed the wide rough water of the Nile twice in the last twenty-four hours, and here they were, off again, leaving well-earned rest and shelter just as evening was falling. But they were still beaming. Never a dull moment, their faces seemed to say.

As for Hilary, his back view as he disappeared into the shadows of the cultivation was the back view of Young Explorer Leading Followers in Gallant Race against Time—Will They Win Through? He *did* know how to enjoy life.

The rest of us had supper almost in silence, John's main contribution to the fun being a sepulchral calculation that the two cables would probably cost about as much as thirty tourieh men working a full day. There didn't seem to be any answer to that one.

The next few days were black. We were getting badly tired; and the irritation which we had felt with George, and which we had tried to suppress, knowing at heart that being what he was, he really couldn't help not being any use, became aggravated by this parting shot of his into something like cold fury. It suddenly brimmed over and reacted amongst ourselves. The fact that he had gone didn't seem to help. Nobody said very much, but what was said was pretty curt. I think, too, that we were suffering from an anti-climax over the hoard of gold and silver. It had been exciting, but couldn't bring the sustained exhilaration which a find of true archaeological value or beauty would have done. Actually it was more of an embarrassment than anything else.

Tommy alone seemed fairly serene. The more funny little bits of baked clay and sherds you could find him—so long as they had inscriptions or fragments of inscriptions on them—the happier he became. While there was always the chance and the hope of a fragment which bore an inscription giving fresh historical knowledge, the bulk of his material consisted of day-to-day happenings—sealings for oil and wine and food-jars; sometimes a letter from one official to another. He had just deciphered a painted clay-sealing from a wine-jar, which read: 'Wine of the Royal House, very, very good.' After each long day on the dig, he slipped away to the small room where the numbered boxes of small dark clay fragments were stacked, and where his notebooks were spread out, filled with long, incredibly neat columns of copied hieroglyphs, transcriptions and translations alongside. Perhaps he watched the ups and downs of the season with the same detachment that he brought to bear on the long ago, tiny goings-on of Akhenaten's City, saw us as just another phase of its history, interesting to contemplate, but as ephemeral as all the rest of it. Perhaps this accounted for the degree of unrufflement he attained.

John showed his fatigue by working even harder than ever, and becoming very silent and dreadfully polite. Hilda was worrying about him. I felt sure that Ralph was running a temperature again, but he refused to have it taken. Hilary slogged round the North Suburb, and muttered in his beard. The dust got into everything, and I had used my last shampoo.

There were only ten days left. Already a tiny wrinkled carpenter from Guft was at work in the courtyard, putting together cases for transporting the season's finds to Cairo. And the word Division came more and more into what now passed for conversation among us. According to the terms of the concession which gave permission to dig, all the finds had to be taken to the Cairo Museum at the end of the season and laid out for inspection. The Department of Antiquities, in the person of the Director of the Museum and his advisers, had the right to take anything which was considered unique, and which, therefore, added to the value of the Museum collections; and after that divide what remained with the excavator. So that a Field Director could be fairly certain in advance that he would be saying good-bye to any spectacular or highly valuable find as soon as he got it to Cairo. For himself he would have the satisfaction of having found it, the sole right of publication on behalf of the Society he worked for, and all the photographs he wanted for that publication. But in a Society like ours, where funds for excavations were uncertain, it was vital to bring back all we could to London. There's nothing like the object itself, on display at the annual exhibition, for attracting attention and increasing interest, and possibly, therefore, subscriptions. It is awfully hard for the layman at an exhibition of antiquities, to work up enthusiasm over a photograph with the depressing little phrase 'Retained in Cairo' added to its descriptive label. So that while we recognized the right of a great National Museum to keep the unique objects from the ancient sites of its own country which excavators of all kinds of nationalities were busy salvaging, we couldn't help hoping passionately, all the same, that the Director would interpret the antiquity law as leniently as possible when it came to our turn. For the law was loosely enough constructed to admit of widely differing interpretations, according to the personality of the Director of Antiquities; there was play within its frame for the human element to count. What was a unique object, after all, where everything was handmade? A rigid Director might say, with truth: 'All these things, except the objects actually made in moulds, are handmade, and therefore unique—we already have two thousand fishhooks, but this one is slightly longer than the rest, so we must have it too.' On the other hand, he *might* say: 'We've got a whole series of statuettes all really very like this one you've found, so you can keep it,' and release a real treasure to the excavator.

John had kept this human element in mind throughout the season in his relations with the Department of Antiquities. Mr. Engelbach, the official who had entertained us in Cairo, and who would probably be present at the Division, advising the Director of the Museum as to what should be retained or released, had been very fierce about the way some digs complied with the regulation that reports and photographs should be sent several times during a season to the Museum. Too often he got hurried scrawls, poor photographs, mistakes in references and so on—the implication being, he said, that the request was red-tape foolishness, the sending of the report and photographs a waste of valuable time, and so hurled rather peevishly at his head.

With this to go on, John saw to it, partly with his tongue in his cheek, partly with an eye quite unashamedly to its possible effect on the Division, and partly because he really intended to run a model dig anyway, and loved neatness and method for its own sake, that our reports to Cairo were frequent, regular and miracles of clarity. He selected above-average prints to go with the report, while I checked and rechecked all his references to them and put on my most pernickety standard of typing for this fortnightly effort. So far, this had worked beautifully. We gathered that the Department was purring over our filial behaviour, and that John was its blue-eyed boy. Whether all this would have the slightest effect on the Division, the next fortnight would show.

Meanwhile the struggle to get through the planned work went on. John had modified his original scheme, and had ruled out the north-east corner of the North Suburb until the following season. He hated making the decision, but remarked philosophically that it would make a further strong argument for urging the committee to find the funds somehow for another expedition in the autumn. "It's so tied up with what we're doing this year that it obviously must be completed before we can publish the whole Suburb," he said.

The carpenter was making six cases: one enormously strong one for the lintel, two for the bird painting (one to go inside the other to minimize jolts), and three more big ones for all the other finds.

It was a distracting morning. I was alone up at the house, beginning to draw up typed lists of all the objects, according to their groups, for use at the Division. The tiny carpenter kept bounding into the office, like a locust in a nightgown, taking the measurements of the lintel where it stood propped against a wall. Then he would patter out and squat down to his work, and the sawing and hammering would begin again, and also sad little Coptic hymns—or they may have been the latest smash hit-tune from Guft for all I knew—the effect would have been much the same in either case, judging from my experience of Egyptian singing to date; a wavering line of long-drawn, almost slurred notes.

The end of the season. Division lists—packing-cases—the wailing melancholy voice in the courtyard mingling with the hammering—and down at the dig the straining routine of the daily work among the grey rubble and flying dust. This morning the magic had gone out of it all somehow, and I felt flat, stale and unprofitable.

I was thankful when Hussein came in to say that the lunch was just going down to the dig; would I be going, or would I have something up here? Unwillingly I said that I would stay up. I longed to get away from the din outside, and the office, and the dull job which I could see would take the rest of the day to do. But unless I was wanted on the dig, my business was to stay and get these lists ready as soon as possible, well before the packing-up began; for all the objects had to be checked against them. Much as I thought I should welcome an interruption, it would only mean that this job would still loom ahead, looking ten times more formidable just so long as it remained untackled; and much more likely to harbour inaccuracies in its long columns of numbers if done at the end of the day, when I, half-asleep, and the oil lamp swaying overhead, contrived between us to make a 3 look like an 8, or the other way round. It needed a fresh eye and a good light to get all these hundreds of figures correct.

As soon as I had grumpily told myself all this, and was morosely eating scrambled eggs in the living-room, wondering if the hammering would have sent me insane by the evening, on the principle of a Chinese torture, a message arrived from the dig that I was wanted down there as soon as possible, with lots of small boxes and brushes. Immediately I became furious at being dragged away from the office. Why couldn't I be left to get on with my proper job? How did they expect to have the office side done efficiently if the secretary was always standing on her head in a duststorm, etc. etc.?

I set off for the dig a few minutes later, bristling with little cardboard boxes and grievances.

And as always—as soon as I found myself off to the dig, swinging over the humps and hillocks with my shoes full of sand, the magic began to work again, smoothing away the petty irritation which was threatening to get out of hand with all of us and shiver to pieces the whole cool vision of our purpose.

I felt better. For one thing it was blessedly quiet after the hammering; and I suddenly noticed that the wind had quite dropped; the sky was clear and the sun bright, the shadows once again clean and sharp along the edge of the cultivation, instead of the blurred grey which we had lately grown to know and hate.

I knew perfectly well that I wouldn't have been interrupted in what I was doing, unless I was really needed for some good reason down at the dig. It was worth being tired and a bit overworked when one knew that it came about through being a vital, if small, part of a purposeful machine.

Someone was coming up from the dig. It was Ralph, and long before he reached me I gathered that he meant, once again, to spend his shoe-sole in dancing round the Maypole.

"Are you feeling better?" I asked rather unnecessarily, as we met.

He had tipped his hat back again at a silly angle, and looked brown and gay.

"I suddenly felt all right again this morning," he said. "For about the first time for over a month. And I've practically finished off my lot of surveying—with luck now I think I see daylight at last—I'm going up to draw now."

"I'm terribly glad, Ralph," I said. "I hope the carpenter won't bring on a relapse. By the way, do you know why I'm wanted down here?"

"I think it's more necklaces," he said. "Hilda was working on one lot, and then they found another patch, just before lunch—hence the S.O.S. I haven't been over there, but I think it's the small house T.36.68. Au revoir—I believe I'll live to see Greece after all."

He went off smiling, and I marched on. We had discovered during the season that we both nursed a lifelong ambition to get to Greece somehow or other. And at Amarna, through John's enthusiastic support and help, this amorphous idea had suddenly become perfectly simple and clearcut. We now had a plan to sail to Athens at the end of the season with introductions from John to the people at the British School of Archaeology, and from there set out for the roadless heart of the country, where our ways would be muletracks threading plain and valley and mountain. John had worked out on paper possible walks for us—Corinth, Mycenae, Tiryns, Epidaurus; perhaps Olympia; or along the slopes of Parnassos to Delphi . . . the dream names glittered as he wrote.

One of the reasons for my own ill-humour lately had been the thought that Ralph wouldn't be in a fit state after his mysterious fevers for such strenuous walks as these clearly would be; he might want only to go straight back to England as soon as possible, and let the whole plan fall through. So I arrived on the dig a few minutes later feeling happier than I'd been for days; and as I began work on the rubble heap near the one that Hilda was just finishing, all the old excitement welled up afresh.

It was a large heap, and Hilda began working on one side of it while I cleared from the top. Single beads and pendants were scattered everywhere but there were no continuous stretches of necklace. We picked them out in scores.

The afternoon wore on and the heap had been reduced to a foot or so above ground level, when my brush moved over something curved and hard; perhaps a big stone. I blew away the sand, and saw a grey-white ridged surface, with flecks of black paint; certainly not a stone. Hilda leaned over and looked. "Try getting the stuff away from the front," she said. "We ought to get a look at it from another angle, before it's moved." I came round and began brushing and blowing at the vertical side of the heap. Down trickled the sand between the harder bits of mud brick, like tiny yellow waterfalls, and nearer and nearer I came to the side of the buried object. A final gentle stroke with a brush tip, and the whispering sand slid away from the surface—and we could see more of the grey and white ridges, and beneath it a smooth curve of reddish-brown paint. The sand had poured away below it and left a cavity. "Can you see inside the hollow?" Hilda asked. I lay down flat and got one eye as close as I could to the rubble.

And then I suddenly saw what the brownish paint was— part of a small face. I could just see the curved chin and the corner of a darker painted mouth. Hilda knelt up and beckoned to John, who was not far away.

"It's the head of a statue, I think," she said quietly as he joined us. He took a long look, and then sat back on his heels. His face was very compressed and tense.

"I'll wait while you get it out," was all he said.

Infinitely slowly we cut back the caked rubble in which it was embedded. The hardest thing on earth is to go slow when you are excited. But we had to—we could never tell how strong or how fragile a find was until it was finally detached from its hiding-place. For all we knew there might be a crack right across the unseen face, so that the whole thing might crumble into powder at a clumsy movement.

We widened the cavity just beneath it, so that John could get his fingers into it in case the head dropped suddenly. He held them there unmoving for at least five minutes, while we worked round the top. "It's coming," he said suddenly.

Hilda blew once more at the surface, and the head sank on to John's hand. He drew it slowly away from the debris. Then very gently he turned the head over on his palm.

Framed by a dark ceremonial wig, the face of a young girl gazed up at us with long, beautifully modelled eyes beneath winging dark eyebrows. The corners of the sweet, full mouth drooped a little. The childish fullness of the brown cheeks contrasted oddly with the tiny determined pointed chin. Somehow the sculptor had caught the pathetic dignity of youth burdened with royalty. The little head was another exquisite example of the genius of the sculptors of Akhenaten's day for perceiving more than the surface truth, and expressing to perfection what they had seen.

I looked up from the head to John's face. In those few moments it had completely lost its gaunt grey look of the past few weeks. He knelt there in the dust, brown and radiant, looking down at the beautiful thing on his hand.

"Now," he said slowly, "our season has been crowned."

Chapter Twelve

THAT evening the sky beyond the motionless trees flamed rose and gold with the promise of more calm days to come; and the Nile was marvellously quiet again. The lamp was already lit when Hilda and I came into the living-room after locking up the medicine cupboard. John had the little head on the table alongside a book open at a photograph of one of the chairs found in Tutankhamun's tomb. The others were round him, and we joined them. On the wooden back of the chair there is a very beautiful scene wrought in sheet gold and silver and costly stones and coloured glass, showing the young Pharaoh seated, leaning casually back, one bent arm hitched over the back of his chair. He is looking gently at his little Royal wife, Ankhsenpaaten, third daughter of Akhenaten. She stands before him, leaning a little forward, rather confidingly, with her right hand gently touching, perhaps patting, his shoulder. John turned the limestone head so that it showed exactly the same view as that in the picture—the left profile.

The likeness was astonishing: the same long eye and dark eyebrow; the same delicate nose; the full mouth, with the little droop where the young cheek curved over towards the small pointed chin. The wigs too were identical in shape.

"I think she *must* be Ankhsenpaaten," John said finally. "I wonder whether people will agree with me."

He shut the book, and suddenly said: "My Majesty requires beer!" It was a long time since we had heard that imperial cry. It told us a lot. It told us that the bad spell was over. It was like rain after drought, sunshine after fog, a train running out of a long tunnel—all sorts of things. It meant that John was happy

149

again; so that *we* could be happy again, for we knew that he must have weighed up the happenings of the season, good and ill, and found the balance well in our favour.

It was a wonderful evening. We sat round the table before supper and drank beer, and passed the small head in its cradle of cotton wool from one to the other, and marvelled at the skill which had expressed so much on so small a scale.

Ralph began to make a drawing of her, and if I needed any proof that he was really fit, I had it now. His eyes looked very blue again, and intrigued and gay. I began to think of mountain peaks, perhaps snowcapped, rising one beyond another; and of Delphi hidden somewhere in their folds.

I looked round the table, and thought of our first night here, nearly four months ago. Outwardly there wasn't much difference, except that now we were all very sunburned. But inwardly . . . we'd been gay then; but it was the polite cautious jollity of untried isolated strangers, each preoccupied a bit perhaps, with individual nervousness about how it was all going to work out. Now it was the best kind of gaiety, coming from deep down, born of a sense of good work struggled through together, and of knowledge that the aching tiredness no longer mattered now that the bad patch of dull depression seemed all at once behind us.

"I shall photograph her tomorrow," John said, "and make a few prints here for the report, so that we can send it quickly. It'll be very interesting trying to get the most out of that subtle modelling; mainly a matter of lighting."

There was little registration that evening, and after it was finished I went off to the office and began again on the Division lists. But the morning mood which I had expected to find even darker if I had to come back to this monotonous piece of work at the end of a long tiring day, had dissolved like mist in the sun. The fresh life and serenity which the little princess had brought into the camp seemed to be penetrating into the most humdrum chores. At this late hour I felt far more wide awake, much more eager to rush at this job and polish it off, than I had in the morning light. I decided to work through at least the bronze and stone groups that evening, including the fragments of sculpture and our new treasure.

It was very late when I came to an end of these groups. The others had all disappeared to their rooms when I finally closed down the office, realizing that, however exhilarated I might be, I was by now properly fagged out. As I passed the dark doorway of the living-room, impulse made me turn in and have one more look at the head of the princess. There she lay in her soft white bed, a faintly smiling look in the long eyes and gentle mouth, as I picked her up in my hand and moved the electric torch slowly from side to side to catch once again, from the shadows it threw, the perfection of the modelling.

Hatiay's lintel had been interesting, the hoard of gold exciting; but it was only now that I knew the true exhilaration that comes from literally unearthing a treasure which in one flash eliminates time; when the ancient artist speaks direct through his creation to all those coming after, who understand his language.

I thought of Alfred Turner: 'Look at all the sculpture you can out there—wish I could see some Egyptian sculpture in its own place—not always in museums.' And I thought of the Central School, and of my own tentative dabbing at clay and chipping at stone. I knew well the difference between average talent and the work of a master when I saw it. I felt very humble. Yet I think my own struggles in the same craft gave me a special insight into the skill of that long dead artist. I'd tried so hard myself to express in clay and stone the living bone formation beneath the softness of flesh and muscle. I knew from my own experience how much observation, how much sensitivity, how much skill must be there to carve a head which convinces that bones really lie beneath the surface, the unseen strength and framework of the whole; it's easy enough to produce a superficial mask, a slick portrait with nothing behind it. And I knew, too, that even when a crafts-man had gained that degree of excellence, the creative work of a true artist might still be beyond him. That ultimate gift —the mysterious gift of expressing the metaphysical in inanimate clay or stone—lies somewhere in the depths of the artist himself, and can neither be imparted nor learned. But here in my hand lay the flowering of both skills—and looking down at the small head, I, a student-apprentice, saluted my unknown artist-craftsman, dead these three thousand years and more.

The wonder of touching something that had lain buried and unmoving for so long came over me again, just as I'd felt when I was new to all this, four months ago. But I'd found that to say: 'This was made three thousand years ago' now hardly stirred my sense of time at all. But I thought of it this way: the little head, wedged in that rubble, up against a ruined wall in this silent, sunny place in Egypt, had been lying there, face downwards, while Troy was burning; while Sennacherib was ransacking the cities beyond his borders; on through the slow centuries, while the greatness of Athens came and went, and while Christ lived out his days on earth. It was still lying there when the Romans first marched on London, when Harold fell at Hastings, and the last Plantagenet at Bosworth Field. On and on through the years, until this hot afternoon when the brush and knife came nearer and nearer to it through the yielding rubble, until it stirred, dropped, and lay once again cupped in a warm human hand.

Perhaps it was just fantasy born of lightheadedness—the late hour, fatigue, and this strange feeling of time being at once an immense thing and yet, somehow, of little importance; but as I stood there in the dark inner room, the tiny spotlight trained on the crowning find of our season, I felt as if a thin wraith were lingering in the courtyard that night, who had herself once held this portrait of a loved daughter in a small brown hand; one who swayed in the night breeze, resting amused eyes through the open doorway on my preoccupation.

I laid the head back, and went through the darkened rooms out into the silvery courtyard. A cool air stirred round me for a moment like the touch of a trailing kirtle—a faint sound, like a small sandalled foot slipping by, died away with the breeze. Then all was moonlight and silence, but for the thin faraway cries of the jackals, sounding like the mournful ghosts of the people who, with the lady Nefertiti, once lived here.

I finished the Division lists the next day. The packing of all the objects was to begin the day after that, a few days before we were to leave. So I asked John if I could try and make cuttle-fish casts of one or two of the metal objects before they were packed, as some of them would certainly be kept in Cairo.

"Cuttlefish casts," he repeated, looking a little dazed.

I explained that I had brought out enough dried cuttlefish in one of my suitcases to start a canary farm.

"Canary farm," he said. "Go on—I'm doing my best."

"But not for canaries," I said. "Casts. It's a technique used by jewellers—in fact, it was a London jeweller who put me up to this and gave me the outfit, and showed me how. He said that if I could make a lead cast of any small objects we found, he would make replicas for us from it, in the same material as the original; but it would have to be something not too fragile."

John became intrigued. We went into the antiquity room, and looked through the objects.

"The Hittite amulet from the hoard," he said. "What about that? I think Cairo is sure to swipe it; it would be awfully nice to have copies of *him*."

"It should be quite strong enough," I said. "It's a solid little thing. You have to put a certain amount of pressure on the thing you are casting, though—it would be frightful if I broke it."

He looked dubious, but said he was prepared to risk it; so I set to work.

The inside of dried cuttlefish is like dazzling white chalk. The technique is to rub two halves together until the surfaces are completely smooth and flat. Then you take them apart and place the object you are casting on one half near one end. I put the amulet down sideways, his beaky nose in profile; then, supporting the outer curve of the fish with one hand in case it broke, I put my thumb on the amulet, and very slowly, very carefully, pressed it down into the chalky bed until it was half submerged. I put the other half of the fish over it and pressed the two pieces together until the flat surfaces met. Four thin, sharp rods like knitting needles were skewered through from front to back at various points to ensure that the two halves would come back in exactly the same position after being taken apart. I took the rods out and lifted off the top half, and very gingerly winkled the amulet out of its cranny. Much to my relief he was no worse for the experience.

Each half of the cuttlefish now carried an exact mould of half the amulet; for the chalky substance was soft enough to allow an object to be pressed into it, but yet hard enough to hold every detail sharp and clearcut.

With a penknife I hollowed out a small funnel about an inch long from the base of the mould to the bottom edge of the fish. Then from the head of the little hollow figure I cut two thin grooves through the chalk away to either edge of the fish. These would act as air-vents to prevent an airlock when the lead was poured in. After this the two halves were laid together again, and the four rods put back through the same holes as before, and held firm with wire twisted from front to back.

Hilary had gallantly sacrificed a few of his cartridges for this experiment and was melting the lead down for me. We up-ended the wired-up cuttlefish between two piles of books and poured the molten lead down the hollow I had cut. There was a faint sizzling. After a few minutes we opened up the con-traption. The white of the chalk round the cast was scorched brown from the heat. And out of the mould we picked the new amulet—an exact replica, except for two thread-like antennae of lead, which had run a little way along the air-vents from the top of the amulet's head. I cut them off with a sharp knife, and also the bit that had solidified below the base in the opening, and the job was done.

Later on, my London jeweller made many charming little reproductions from this lead cast, the bodies of solid silver, the round caps of gold, just like the original. One of them faces me at this moment.

The following morning Hilda and I began packing all the small objects. They were laid in cardboard boxes, well padded with cotton wool, and had their serial numbers recorded on the lids; and by teatime they were ready to be packed down into the three big cases standing out in the hot courtyard. Our mood was one of gentle melancholy, alternating with one of gentle apoplexy as we stood on our heads settling the first boxes on to the bottom padding.

By the evening all that remained unpacked were the lintel and the bird painting. John arrived with several of the Guftis, and they trundled the lintel into its huge flat case on rollers, one long side having been left off until this was done. Then we lined the inner case which had been made for the bird fragment with a thick layer of cotton wool; to minimize jarring, this inner case was to be entirely insulated from the outer one by straw and tight rolls of newspaper. But even so I felt sure that the hammering on of the lids, however gently done, would jar the fragile painting dangerously. So when the carpenter began whanging on the lids of the other cases, John let me fix both the outer and inner lids of these two cases with screws. As the outer lid was fastened down, we wondered if all this rather experimental effort would be effective, and whether we should ever see our pretty bird again.*

That evening Ralph and Hilary rolled up all their season's work—the plans and sectional drawings of every house which had been dug and cleared, and the architectural details of each house, including the elevations and reconstructions of some of them—and sealed them into metal cylinders; and gave me lists to type of what each cylinder contained.

Once again the antiquity room was as empty as we had first found it. Out in the moonlight the sturdy cases gleamed trim and white among the litter of straw and paper. Another season was coming full circle.

A big sailing barge arrived at our landing-stage the next afternoon to ship the cases the two hundred odd miles down to Cairo. The local workmen all turned up, partly to help man-handle the cases on board, and partly for the fun of it. It wasn't often that such a large vessel tied up on this side of the river. It was like the greatgrandfather of our own felucca, enormously bigger, but with just the same air of wild improvisation combined with squat solidity; repairs and patches of every kind and colour of wood banged on all over the place. It looked at one and the same time as if it might sink without warning, and yet, somehow as if it never would. It might have been hundreds of years old—perhaps it was. I thought of Flecker: 'A drowsy ship of some yet older day. . . .'

One by one the cases were brought down from the house, and made the last hazardous few feet up the crazy gang-plank. The lintel came last, this time riding on only two long poles, running fore and aft, the only way of navigating it through the narrow tree-shaded path. When all the cases were safely on

* It was, and we did.

board, the three Guftis who were going to escort them on the three-day trip to Cairo, and see them safely the short distance from the river bank there to the back entrance of the Museum, came primly down the path in single file, staves in one hand, little bundles in the other; in single file they gravely mounted the gang-plank; tall, slim, black-gowned and white-turbaned, a look of Shem, Ham and Japheth about them, a look of 'this isn't our line, really'. We should see them again four days later in Cairo, so there were no elaborate farewells. They were greeted gaily by the gap-toothed old salt in charge of the craft, and the crew of three, large beaming young men who may have been his grandsons.

Once the cases were settled in a solid evenly-balanced mass round the foot of the mast, no time was lost in getting under way. Ropes were cast off, and Shem, Ham and Japheth helped to haul them in and coil them down, precise as ever in a detached unnautical way, while the crew poled the great clumsy craft away from the bank, with shouts of laughter and banter hurled at the ribald landlubber villagers left on shore. We watched them drifting further and further out, and before long we could see that Ham had rolled up his sleeves, could hear that Shem was singing, and the staid Japheth laughing at something the old captain had said. It seemed as if the holidays were really beginning, when even prefects unbend; and as if there was something about a sailor that even a Gufti couldn't resist.

Now as they stood well out from shore they began to unfurl the two sails, with their curious rig—they fanned out almost horizontally on either side of the mast, like the wings of a gigantic bird. And as the gentle breeze took and filled them, the old ship changed under our eyes from a clumsy joke into a lovely thing of gleaming beauty. Away it floated across the quiet water, and as it met the mid-river current, the prow turned slowly northward, the sails shivered, swung and filled again, leaning a little into the first long tack against the eternal breeze from the north; the long journey had begun.

The locals had drifted away by now in small groups to the village, laughing and chattering; but we lingered on the bank and watched the season's finds out of sight. The shining wings above the strange cargo were now abreast of the north headland; a few minutes more and they would have passed beyond it. I thought of the head of the princess; of the carefully threaded gleaming necklaces; of the bronze knives and mirrors; of Hatiay's glowing lintel, which once he had raised with such pride above the best doorway in his fine new house; all moving away down river for ever from the place where they belonged, where they had lain so long.

As the white sails slipped out of sight, no one said a word; but we all knew then that at that moment the season was over.

"I think," said John, after a pause, but still looking at the headland, and the stretch of blank blue water lying at its foot, "we'll have a fantasia tonight."

The news was quickly sent round that all who could sing and dance and all who would like to watch were welcome up at the house that evening. Hussein and Young Abu Bakr set lanterns high up round the courtyard, and a row of camp chairs along the wall of the living-room. While we were having

supper we were conscious of a growing murmur, and rustling movements outside; an occasional experimental twitter on a pipe or thump on a drum; and Hussein had a look of suppressed excitement about him as he slid round the table, handing the dishes.

When we emerged we could see the soft lights falling on the

dark faces of all the workmen and most of their families, pressed in a great throng up against the outer wall. A man and two of our laundry girls squatted by the kitchen door, each with a great drum nursed under one arm. The drums were made of pottery, hollow and funnel-shaped, with a strong circle of animal skin lashed over the large end. Two men sat near them crosslegged, with long bamboo pipes in their hands.

A boy laid a bundle of straw in front of the drummers and lit it. They held the drums towards the blaze and tapped on the skins which tightened in the warmth, so that the note of the tapping rose swiftly. We settled in our chairs, and the drummers beat out a strange rhythm, now together, now in a kind of stammering argument. It was not only rhythmical but actually varied in notes, like a weird tune, for this trio were experts and could draw different sounds at will from the skins by varying the place and manner of their beats; a deep thrilling boom coming from a strong blow in the centre, and a much higher, lighter, delicate sound from the fingers of the other hand tapping swiftly at the circumference.

Their hands were wonderful to watch; moving from the wrists alone, supple yet steely; arms motionless as they cradled the heavy funnels.

Now the pipers joined in, and a shiver of delight went through the waiting crowd. Both had a drone pipe, and while their fingers moved over the stops of the tune pipe, the drones began to fill the air, matching the deep steady beat of the drums. For a few minutes they all played as if feeling towards each other, tentatively ; but soon they seemed no longer five different people grouped round the small glowing fire. They had fused into one great sound which was becoming over-powering and irresistible. They played as one man—here was no amorphous improvised tune, vaguely wavering from one quartertone to another, as till now I had imagined their music to be whenever I'd heard it. Every rise and fall, every shake

and grace-note came in unison from the two pipers, and was echoed and given point and depth by the skill of the drummers, sitting like images with their eyes cast down over their nimble fingers. The wailing pipes and the throbbing drums—the lamp-light and firelight flickering over the massed intent faces of the villagers, fallen under the spell of their own folk music—and over it all, the wheeling, jewelled sky; one of the moments which stay with you a lifetime.

They had all quite forgotten us; perhaps because by now they had almost accepted us as part of their own life. For this was no longer our party to which they had been bidden; it was as if we had been admitted into the real life of Egypt this evening, as we, along with them, were drawn deeper and deeper into the hypnotic ecstasy of the weaving music.

Hussein stood quietly by us; but his eyes were strangely hooded, his great hands patting gently together. The villagers stood completely silent; but the silence held a mounting tension.

Then suddenly a white-clad figure broke through the gap in the wall and stood alone in the courtyard before us. The moment had come when a singer could keep silent no longer. A stir, and smiling faces showed that the tension had relaxed a little.

"The best singer in the villages," Hussein whispered happily, back in his own skin again. "You cannot make him sing if he does not wish."

The man was no longer young and his clothes were ragged, but he stood there quietly, head thrown back, as one in authority, aware of his power to sway his fellows at the first sound of his voice. His hand came up to the side of his mouth, cupping it as if to carry his notes to the far end of Egypt. And then his golden voice joined the pipes and drums; and the musicians, true artists saluting a master, sank their clamour to a whisper, and let the beautiful voice soar away high and clear above them. I couldn't understand the words; but Hussein leaned over and said that it was a very, very old song—about a king's young son who was drowned in a river at harvest time.

The villagers swayed to his song, and groaned as he groaned at the end of each repeated chorus line; and the pipes softly echoed the lament, and the drums spoke of sorrow and loss and the end of all things.

Silence at last; and then the singer bowed his head and sank down by the fire, and leaned towards it as if exhausted; just raising one hand to acknowledge the burst of acclamation on every side as soft, quick clapping broke out, and ejaculations of wonder filled the air. He lit a cigarette and leaned back against the kitchen wall, smiling a little, withdrawn.

Now into the courtyard sprang lithe Mahmud Umbarak, the Gufti, and began very seriously an intricate dance. It was mostly neat footwork, watched with passionate attention by

161

the villagers; but at the same time he made slow beautiful movements with his arms, now sweeping his white staff about his turbaned head, now holding it along his shoulders in small delicate fingers. The foot movements were so precise and neat that his blackrobed figure seemed to be gliding about the court-yard, like a ballerina on her points, his body swaying very slightly under the wheeling mesmeric beauty of his white wand. But there was no emotional strain here—only the eye was enslaved; all was pure abstract movement. The austerity of the Guftis seemed epitomized here, as Mahmud, the lashes of his downcast eyelids almost resting on the high cheekbones, gravely and beautifully circled the courtyard, intent only on the tech-nical perfection of his dance. Again, warm delighted applause broke out as his performance ended, and he slipped away.

One turn after another followed, and it grew late. Three girls danced together; and then a tumbler ran round on his hands with coloured handkerchiefs nipped between his up-turned grotesquely waving toes. Round him jigged two men carrying coloured handkerchiefs in both hands which they alternately waved round their heads and then flicked downward and then behind them. Where had I seen just that step and just those arm movements before? Ralph suddenly said: "It's Morris Dancing." Of course. I'd last seen exactly this under a pale Essex sky at Thaxted.

"I believe Morris is a corruption for Moorish," said John. "So we're probably seeing something like the origin of it all here and now. The Moors must have taken it with them all the way from Arabia proper to Europe; or perhaps the Crusaders brought it back to England."

I watched the dark fantastic figures leaping in the lamplight, the handkerchiefs twirling and sinking—and in my mind's eye saw the fair young men in flannels, gay with garters and bells and coloured kerchiefs, leaping in an English May Day revel. How many more of our customs, I wondered, which we think of as essentially English, had roots tapering away like this to Arabia or even beyond?

The music stopped and the dancers hopped and jigged gaily away, to be met with laughter and affectionate thumps on the back from their friends.

Suddenly the Funny Man appeared from nowhere, and straddled before us, posturing and gesturing. He was one of the great characters on the dig, and was always known amongst ourselves as the Funny Man, although I think his name was Khalifa. He was a natural comic, a good-hearted kindly clown, whose near neighbours on the dig, as they dug and shovelled round him, always seemed to be in stitches.

Now he began to stagger round the courtyard, clutching his head and trembling in every limb, apparently an old, ill man; and then another of the workmen crept into the arena, stalking him silently in the shadow of the walls, until the Funny Man suddenly caught sight of him. Then he leaped into the air with fright, and forgetting his simulation of tottering senility, began to play the clown in good earnest, leaping the column bases, howling and gibbering, bounding backwards and forwards over the courtyard parapet, while we and the entire audience rocked with laughter.

The end came—the attacker was too much for him—whacks on the head brought him to the ground, and then his assailant finished him off as he lay, and danced away out of the courtyard. The Funny Man tried hard to sham dead for about half a minute; but there were twitches and winks and kicks and mutterings which produced the laughter which he simply couldn't resist playing for. But all the same, Hussein told us firmly, he was quite, quite dead.

The other actor came slowly back. This time he had a shawl over his head which hid most of his face, and his whole attitude was drooping and sorrowful. "Now he is the dead one's wife," said Hussein. "She is looking for him." Round the courtyard the sad figure moved, carefully not seeing the lighthearted corpse spread out in full view, and irrepressibly wisecracking. Then came the dreadful discovery; and the cloaked figure dropped on its knees and rocked backwards and forwards inconsolably in the moonlight. "Now she has found him," Hussein explained kindly.

A third actor moved forward from the shadows, and the crowd fell curiously quiet. He wandered about the courtyard, one arm curved round as if it held an invisible basket. The other hand dipped continuously into this hollow and then was flung outwards, now to the front and now to the side, over and over again.

John suddenly sat up very straight. "He's sowing seed," he whispered very quietly, but full of excitement. "This is *incredible*. I believe they're doing a sort of pantomime version of an old corn-spirit ritual."

At last the imaginary shower of seed fell upon the dead man. His wife sprang up and began to dance round him, raising arms on high as if in supplication. The body began to roll to and fro, and groan; and laughter came again from the crowd, but raggedly, uncertainly, for now they were touched with something like awe—it seemed as if they knew they were watching some great crisis which they themselves shared in, as if it lay somewhere deep in their own hearts, a subconscious, nameless memory.

Quickly the dead man gathered strength and vitality and rose to his feet. Then he began to caper about on one of the column bases, shouting words of joy, his face turned up to the stars. Then hopping off, he took his wife's hands and they danced triumphantly round the courtyard, and so away, followed by the sower.

It was late now. Everyone seemed to take for granted that the strange little mime was the climax of the entertainment. John stood up, and the band stood up too, and played a final stirring tune. Then he went towards the wall, the lamplight shining on his bare head and the blue Cretan cloak. He made a short speech to the throng, and told them that they had made a wonderful evening for us all; that they had worked hard all the season, that it had been a fine season, and he thanked them all—and by God's will we would all come back again soon, and have another fine season.

"By God's will! By God's will! In sh' Allah! In sh' Allah!" came the shouts; and suddenly one of the Guftis called out that there had never been 'a Mudir like his honour the Man'— 'Mudir zey genabbu er Ragil.' They waved and clapped and laughed; and John lifted a hand in quiet acknowledgement, then turned and came past us and went into the living-room, flushed and perhaps a little tremulous. When we joined him he said: "That's the highest honour I've ever had, or ever hope to have"—and then softly, almost to himself, repeated smiling: "Genabbu er Ragil."

Hussein came in with beer and sandwiches; and John asked him what he knew about the Funny Man's play. He stood in the doorway, tawny eyes gleaming, his face creased with happy smiles, waving his hands as he tried to explain. It was a story *min zamân, min zamân*, from long, long ago. Khalifa was the old man, who had to die to save his people. He was slain by a bad man. He died when the corn was ripe. He stayed dead till the seed was sown and the corn was beginning to sprout.

"Who is that old man, really?" John asked. He hesitated a moment. Then: "Some say he is the maize crop and the corn crop."

"Do *you* think that, Hussein?" He looked very grave. "It is just an old story, min zamân, min zamân."

When he had gone we talked it all over, the whole evening, with its enchanting displays of natural unselfconscious talent; but mainly we discussed the mime. We knew we had been privileged to see something strange and wonderful. Ragged

165

and twisted though this surviving shred might be, grotesque and part-ribald, it yet led straight back to the remote ages. Far back beyond the days of Akhenaten himself, yet still a fibrous reality twisted inextricably into the vitals of these living men of today. We had seen it in Hussein's face, whatever he said; heard it in the sudden hush which had fallen on the rough crowd as they watched the miracle of resurrection—of whom? The eyes which had wrinkled with laughter at the Funny Man's fooling had then grown wide with awe. For they had forgotten for the moment their well-known buffoon—they had seen another lying there in his place, waiting for the seed to fall and sprout; one who was nameless to them by now, almost a legend, min zamân, min zamân—yet deep down he was real, and they knew him; one who had died violently that they might live, who had given his body to be their food, the dying god—Osiris.

Chapter Thirteen

THE last three days fled away. On one we paid off the workmen; on the next we made a last swift tour of the Main City and North Suburb, and appointed the four guards whose duty it would be, all through the summer, to prevent illegal digging for loot.

Then one last rather sad day, packing. The only person who seemed really happy was Hussein, for he had a tremendous jaunt ahead. John had decided not to send the robber's hoard with the other finds; instead, Hussein was to come to Cairo with us, carrying the gold and silver in a strong suitcase, and never letting it out of his sight until we got to the Museum; and then by way of combining business with pleasure, John and Hilda were going to take him round Cairo, which he had never yet seen, before he went south again to close down the Expedition House for the summer.

Now it was time to go. One last look back, before the trees of the cultivation hid it all, at the old house lying in the sun; at the distant tangle of ruins, where already the dust haze of our activity had drifted down and settled, a brown veil drawn over the sleeping city until we should return; at the faraway cleft in the face of the sunbaked cliffs, the gateway to the Valley of the Shadow.

We crossed the peaceful water again, looking back now at the friendly people gathered at the landing-stage. Gradually they dwindled into a small black and white knot, faces no longer recognizable; and yet for a long time we could make out individuals as they stood there waving farewell—the Gufti Hussein Sawag by his headdress, which he always wound so loftily above his high forehead—the Funny Man, by the way he kept darting about, huge arms windmilling—Young Abu Bakr, by the way he stood quite still, a head shorter than all the others, a slim disconsolate midget.

Then at last we turned northward, the old felucca drifting silently except for the rhythmical creak and plop and trickle of the leisurely oars moving through the bright water; we watched the sloping headland as it seemed to slide forward like a great door closing, gradually cutting off the view of the lovely place which had come to be our home.

First it hid the tiny white group still just discernible at the landing-stage. Then the long green line of palms along the shore; until at last the whole of the bay that held Akhenaten's City lay secretly once again behind its golden bastion.

For me the door had closed on something very precious; because I knew that even if I came back many times to this place, it would never again hold quite the same magic. The senses would never again be quite so vulnerable to the impact of its strange beauty. In more prosaic ways perhaps, I might gain; I would know more, make fewer mistakes, talk more easily to the Egyptians, and, altogether, be more useful to the Expedition's work—but at that moment I was only conscious of a sense of loss, for the things that could not be found again, that pass like a morning mist in the sun, never to return; that yet remain vivid in the heart long after the solid facts of daily life are quite forgotten.

At the station our party began to break up. We left Tommy standing on the platform waving us off, surrounded by the felucca boys and the locals who had come to help with the luggage; for he was going south by a later train, to spend some weeks on another dig south of Luxor. One last wave, one last long look at the headland, far away now, hazy in the afternoon heat, and we drew in our heads and closed the windows, just as the first wave of dust swirled up from the moving coach wheels.

There were the coloured photographs above the seats again,

of the Pyramids and the Luxor Palace Hotel, and all the rest of it. The carriage seemed stifling and cramped, and exactly matched our own sensation as we came back to the hedged-about world of the twentieth century. But after a few minutes Hilary helped to cheer us up; he was going on that night, straight through from Cairo to Palestine, and he showed us how he'd hidden a golden sovereign which he always carried about with him, from the eagle eyes of the Customs officials at the frontier. He was quite certain that it would be confiscated on the spot if found on him, and he himself gaoled. He gleefully produced a pot of shaving cream, in which he had first buried the coin, and then had spent ages smoothing over the top to make it look unused. The Lone Hand pitting his wits against Authority.

"Well, I'm glad your shaving cream has come in useful for *something*," said John, who had borne the jungle of beards all round him with fortitude.

Late that evening we reached Cairo. On the platform, totally unexpected and wonderfully cheering to see, stood the three Guftis who had sailed with the finds; a fragment of the life we had left behind still lingered. There was a round of handshaking and greetings. They told us that they had only reached Cairo that morning, but that the cases were now safely at the Museum.

Some of the expensive-looking tourists who had come up on the same train from Assuan and Edfu, from Luxor and Abydos and all the other show places, looked curiously at us as they passed by on their way to the glittering cars at the station entrance which would whirl them away to Shepheard's in time for dinner. What kind of people are these, their glance seemed to suggest? English obviously, from their clothes—but how those clothes need valeting—look as if they'd been folded up for months—and listen to them—chattin' away to the three Gyppos as if they know 'em quite well. That's no way to make the wogs respect us. . . .

It wasn't their fault that probably their only experience of the Egyptian in his own country was either a pestering maddening fellow whining to show them the Pyramids and Temples; or else a sharp little provincial who had passed some exams., and climbed into a black coat and trousers, and was becoming daily more clamorous about the iniquitous British on his soil. They couldn't know anything of the life of the true countrymen of Egypt who remained hidden in the cultivation, hardy peasants, with their own sturdy qualities of loyalty and salty, jeering humour. I saw this, and realized more than ever before how privileged I'd been to have had the chance of plunging right into the heart of Egypt's life, bypassing the tourist world. The sightseeing would come later, but now, luckily, I should never see things quite as a tourist.

We saw Hilary into the night train for Palestine; and off he went hugging his golden secret with his finger metaphorically, as always, to nose.

"Suppose they don't even open any of his luggage?" asked Hilda.

"He'll die of disappointment," said Ralph.

There were only four little nigger boys left now; we left the station still chuckling, but sad as well. Hilary was an endearing soul, and it would be a pity when he began to grow up.

So the long day ended, the only further incident being Hussein's one moment of panic. At the steps of the Continental Hotel he lost sight of us for a moment in the crowd of people passing up and down to the entrance, and along the wide pavement. I think he thought that we had somehow got into the hotel ahead of him, for we saw him suddenly bolt up the gleaming steps clutching the precious suitcase, charge the revolving doors, and begin to follow them round for ever; we reached him as he was setting off on about the sixth revolution, eyes starting out of his head; and managed to extract him before he completely lost control. For a moment he looked crestfallen; but he soon cheered up and began to wrinkle up into laughing delight at his own folly and the wonders of civilization. John took over the suitcase into his keeping for the night, and Hussein went off with the Guftis.

The next day a message came from the Museum that the cases were ready to be unpacked for the Division. We went round at once to Mr. Engelbach's office, and he took us to a large room at the back of the Museum, almost empty except for several long trestle tables. The cases were standing near the tables, with their lids removed.

"Can you get unpacked today?" he asked. "If so, we can have the Division at 10 tomorrow morning. The Old Man is free then, and we've got all your lists—everything seems to be in order."

We said we could. We spent the rest of the day unpacking the finds, and setting them out in groups, each in neat rows, all over the tables. So familiar; and yet already the look of the museum object was creeping over them all in that sterile room.

At the end of the long afternoon Mr. Engelbach came back, and looked the finds over; he had seen photographs of most of them already, of course, so that he knew a good deal about them. When he saw the princess he shook his head.

"I'll do my best for you—but I think the Old Man is *bound* to want that for the Museum; she *is* a dear, isn't she? But you never know—and I'll do what I can, as I say—owe you something for the nice way you've treated us all through the season." John coughed gently, looked down his nose, and trod on my foot all in one movement.

Mr. Engelbach wouldn't commit himself about the identity of the head, but admitted guardedly that she could easily be Ankhsenpaaten.

The next morning the Division took place. The Old Man, in other words, the Director of the Museum, M. Lacau, was a tall elderly Frenchman with a white beard, spectacles worn on the end of his nose, and anxious old blue eyes scanning us over the top. The long morning's work began. He moved infinitely slowly along the tables, with Mr. Engelbach and John on either side, the former expounding in rapid French, John putting in an occasional word where it was needed. Sometimes the Old Man held something up to the light and gazed at it with head thrown back and beard jutting, wonderful long hands turning some small object round and round as if the delicate white fingers alone could tell him its worth. Sometimes all three bent together over something on the table, heads nearly touching. From where I stood watching, following along at a respectful six feet or so, it had the look of some solemn religious ritual, priest and two deacons moving slowly sideways together along a fantastically long altar, bowing and straightening, while the murmuring voices rose and fell.

As they moved on, I moved up, to note down those of the objects which M. Lacau had set aside out of each group for Cairo. (Hatiay's lintel had been seen first and annexed at once.) I had the full list of objects with me, and now checked off on it each object which had been retained for the Museum, with a large 'C' opposite its serial number. Naturally this list contained some of our best finds, and it was a sad business, entering that 'C' and patting the little things good-bye that I'd helped to clean and mend and even excavate. The frog amulet, two fine bronze knives, an alabaster jar with an inscription, a dark blue glazed brick with a beautiful incised design in light blue of lotuses round a pool, a child's toy in the form of a hippopotamus, the best of our necklaces.

The morning wore on, and I seemed to be writing 'C' against a great many of our finds; it didn't look as if we should have much of a display at the summer exhibition. I glanced at John, who seemed quite unruffled; and at Mr. Engelbach, who was getting restive. He dropped back a little and spoke sideways to me.

"He's being rather tough—sorry about it—but there's a lot of interesting stuff here. Still, it isn't over yet."

He moved back, and I went on picking up the retained objects, deciphering their numbers and entering them in the lists. Well, anyway, we'd several very nice things, besides heaps of the better known common objects, the coloured amulets and beads and ring bezels. There was a good, though uninscribed alabaster jar left to us, some very interesting sculptors' trial pieces, a bronze mirror, and a little bronze vanity case with part of some scissors and tweezers in it, and one good necklace.

M. Lacau reached the regimented bars of gold and silver, and gazed at them in mild astonishment. John had thoughtfully arranged them in two well-defined halves. . . . The little gold and silver mascot stood between. The Old Man swooped on the small amulet, while John explained the finding of the Crock of Gold.

"I do not want all the gold and silver," said the Old Man, "but this little man I must have—he is interesting. We will retain one half of your hoard—you may keep the other."

That was better than we had hoped. Now the only first-class object to be considered was the princess head. M. Lacau reached the spot where it lay. He picked it up. The long fingers turned the little head lovingly from side to side.

"Excellent," he said, "I think I must——"

"Surely our series of Amarna portraits is extensive enough, sir?" Mr. Engelbach spoke quietly, but he was getting red in the face.

"We have a fine series, yes," was the response, "but the unusual delicacy of this modelling——"

"It's practically a replica of the sandstone one from two years ago, sir, apart from the wig, is it not? And not so perfect. You notice the chip out of the chin? (Put it *down*, you old rascal.)" This last—in English—was delivered, I need hardly say, in a whisper, but with incredible violence.

There was a long agonizing pause. John gazed out of the window. Mr. Engelbach went quietly purple. I chewed the end off my pencil.

At last: "No, I will not retain this—as my friend says, our series of Amarna sculpture is well represented—I do not think I am justified in retaining this piece as well."

He laid the head back in its box lingeringly, reluctantly; and none of us felt safe till he had moved on and was studying the last few objects. But as far as we were concerned the Division was over; it didn't matter what happened now. We not only had a good deal of averagely interesting material to take back to London, but over and above that we had one very good necklace, half the hoard of gold and silver, and best of all, the princess. It was much better than we had dared hope.

Now it really was at an end. M. Lacau shook hands, expressed the hope that our Society would apply again for the concession to dig the following season, congratulated us on our results, shook hands again, bowed several times from the waist, and retired to his office. Mr. Engelbach sat down on the hindquarters of a small sphinx which happened to be about the place, took off his tarbush and wiped his brow.

"*Do* hope you're satisfied," he said. "He was tetchy at the beginning—I thought he was going to have the lot at one point."

"Completely satisfied," John said, delightedly, "and immensely grateful. We certainly shouldn't have got the head without your persuasive tongue."

"No, I thought that was a goner," he said. "And we really don't need it for the collection—it's of much greater value to you."

Two of the Museum workmen came in with a trolley, and loaded it up with the objects for Cairo; and then it was wheeled away to the Museum workrooms.

The following day we filled up innumerable Customs forms,

repacked the cases, and started the finds on the long journey to London, where, after the summer exhibition, they would all be allocated among the different museums which subscribed to the Society's work.

Perhaps here I may go ahead with them a little way and follow the fortunes of one or two.

The committee later on decided that it was permissible to sell our share of gold and silver, and the Bank of England paid us £200 for it, which was credited to the funds for digging at Amarna the following season. And when this transaction was completed, John's words came echoing back . . . "and meanwhile hope for buried treasure—£200 of it". It had come true —not quite in time for that season, but it did indeed add about three weeks' digging power to the following one.

But before it was sold it took part in the exhibition. We arranged a showcase to look exactly like the scene at the moment when the Crock of Gold had been opened; and it attracted a lot of interest. There was the crock lying on its side in real sand, with the original bars of gold and silver streaming out of its mouth, and a replica in gold and silver of the Hittite amulet, made from my lead cast, standing in the sand in front.

There, too, at the exhibition, of course, was the head of the princess, in pride of place in the centre of the hall. After the exhibition an American lady, who had always given most generously to the Society's work in the field, said that if we would allocate the little head to the Metropolitan Museum of New York when the distribution took place, she would donate £1,000 to the following season's work.

So it was that eventually the hoard found its way into the vaults of the Bank of England; and the princess made one last long journey across the water, and today stands in a showcase in New York.

A young girl, a great artist and a robber—these three people of long ago had secured for us our next season's work.

But I've rushed too far ahead. We were still in Cairo, tired but jubilant. One last dinner together, with a comfortable jumble of conversation which included suggestions for the preparation of the exhibition in June (John and Hilda wouldn't be leaving Crete for England until May)—reminiscences of the good days behind us—scribbled notes and sketch-maps from John giving last-minute information about walking in Greece, the price we should pay for guides, the people we must see, the things we mustn't miss, the best way to reach Delphi . . . and then it was all over.

The next day Ralph and I sailed for Athens.

Epilogue

In 1976, the Egypt Exploration Society renewed its concession to excavate at Tell el Amarna, and work has continued there. But it may be of interest to readers of this book to learn something of the later activities of the people who worked there for the last time, nearly 70 years ago.

Although he was not one of the staff who came to excavate, Hussein Abu Bakr cannot be omitted. He worked for most of his life as head servant of the house on the dig. As a child, while training as a house boy, he had known Flinders Petrie. He spoke no English. His brother was the cook, and between them they ministered to the creature comforts of the staff in a perfectly simple, but quite remarkable way.

The smooth running of the house contributed enormously to the much-needed relaxation after a long, hard day on the dig. But Hussein was far more than an efficient and authoritative houseman – tall for an Egyptian, very dark and dignified, he was our cheerful friend with the welfare of the staff at heart.

John Pendlebury, a fine athlete himself, discovered that Hussein was expert with the Quarterstaff, a primitive form of fencing, and asked him to teach him the rules and movements. They would circle each other, attacking and defending, occasionally yelling an Arabic taunt in mock fury. After the bout, they would go their ways laughing, John perhaps to do some work in the office and Hussein to lay the supper.

Once a week, Hussein went to a Muslim religious gathering at a nearby village on the Nile. He told John once how sad he felt that, since none of us were Muslims, he would never see us again when he reached Heaven.

Now for those who came to excavate. Hilary Waddington eventually grew up and, after working on various digs in Palestine, spent most of his active life attached to the Indian Government's Archaeological Survey, his greatest interest lying in the restoration of ancient temples. He worked hard and successfully there, earning an MBE in 1947. He died in 1989 aged 85.

Ralph Lavers, sensitive, humorous and talented, was a fine architect and draughtsman, not very robust and very slight in build. He became tetchy when less perceptive people (not at Tell el Amarna) mistook him for a nice lad of 16 or so, rather beneath their notice, instead of seeing the mature and thoughtful man he really was. I lost touch with him until I was looking for someone to illustrate this book, and knew he was exactly the person to do it. I think his drawings show clearly his own amused memories of Amarna in his carefully observed figures of the men, boys and girls working on the dig – sadly, he died not long after completing the illustrations.

I do not know why or when 'Tommy' became the nickname of Herbert Fairman, the epigraphist on our expedition. After the war, in 1949, he was appointed to the Brunner Chair of Egyptology at Liverpool, a Professor with an international reputation as a scholar and teacher; to the great good fortune of his students, who found in him just the same cheerful enthusiasm for all things Egyptian as we had witnessed in his youth. During his middle years, he also much enjoyed joining tours to Egypt as a guide/lecturer.

The difficulty of talking to a motley gathering of tourists, so that everybody is interested, is obvious. Some of the flock are already really knowledgeable about Egyptology, some have an amateur smattering of the subject, and some know nothing at all as yet and are, perhaps, humbly hoping for a shred of enlightenment. Some of the last, I know, had come up against the occasional pompous lecturer, who answered their elementary questions curtly, implying clearly that they were wasting his time.

Not so, Tommy. He wanted them *all* to enjoy the tour as much as he did, and treated each and everyone kindly and lucidly, if strenuously. At the end of a hard day's slog, he was inclined to say: 'I think we've *just* got time – if you're not *too* tired – but I simply must show you this. Come on.' And they came on. At the end of his tours, everyone, half dead on their feet, would agree that they had had the best tour ever. Tommy died in 1982, aged 75.

Our Director, John Pendlebury, was also at that time Curator at Knossos, directing the excavations there, still continuing near the Palace, when Sir Arthur Evans, now ageing, was in England. John's wife, Hilda, also a classical scholar, helped him in much of his work aimed at elucidating the many links between Ancient Egypt and Minoan Greece.

I remember when John read out to us a letter from his father telling him that Sir Arthur had just received a gold medal from the Royal Geographical Society for the discovery and excavation, the previous year, of a fine Royal Tomb near the Palace. Hilda exploded: 'It's so unfair! *You* discovered the tomb, *you* excavated it, *you* published the results – and little Arthur gets the medal.'

John smiled gently: 'Why worry? When *I'm* 77, *I* shall be getting all the medals for work done by my underlings.' We all laughed, mercifully ignorant that John would never see his 37th birthday, let alone his 77th.

When the war came, a few years later, he enlisted in the army for special duties. Just after the fall of France to the Germans, in 1940, he was sent to Crete with the status of Vice-consul, but in reality to organise a resistance movement there in anticipation of the almost certain invasion, once Hitler had crushed the Greek mainland. A better man could not have been found to do just that. John was well-known and trusted all over Crete and could speak the varying dialects of people living in obscure villages all over the island.

In the ten months or so before the German invasion began in May, 1941, he succeeded in setting up many guerrilla groups of high efficiency. But he was never able to achieve the full amount of arms and equipment he desperately needed and continually begged for, simply because Britain's military resources at this crucial point in the war were already hopelessly overstretched in every direction.

On 21st May, 1941, the skyborne invasion of Crete, launched from the south of Greece, began. John left his office in Heraklion and, with one of his agents, set out to reach the guerrilla meeting point to the West of the town. They were cut off and surrounded by landing parachutists and John was badly wounded. He was carried to a roadside cottage, the home of another agent, whose wife and sister did what they could for him. German soldiers searched the cottage and took away his identity disc. From this the German officers knew very well who he was, and the next morning the soldiers came back with their orders. One witness told later of John's execution outside the cottage and of his proud bearing at this last scene.

The resistance in Crete went on so stubbornly for many weeks (Hitler had expected to subdue it in a few days) that many people – Hilda among them – dared to hope that he might have escaped to the mountains and still be directing the operation – but, at last, the true story was revealed and confirmed. Hilda went on alone to bring up their two children and lived to see them grow up.

This then is a brief outline of what befell my colleagues and friends who worked throughout the thirties at Tell el Amarna, written by the only survivor. The last few years before the war, I joined a dig in Mesopotamia, doing the same kind of administrative work, but on a much bigger scale. The dig was run by the Oriental Institute of the University of Chicago and its Director was the brilliant Henri Frankfort; the staff was large and friendly, but I never stopped being home-sick for Tell el Amarna.

During the war, I and my bicycle (no petrol available then) got into an argument with a large military lorry – an argument which, not unnaturally, I lost, and which at a stroke put an end to the strenuous activity essential to life on a dig, which I had hoped to resume when the war ended.

I realised I would have to change direction completely. Could I write, perhaps? While recuperating in the summer of 1942, I studied garden birds through field-glasses and tentatively sent a light-hearted piece to the magazine *Punch* called 'Birdwatching' which, to my surprise, was accepted. That gave me hope and I went on writing. Later, I turned to broadcasting: my first talk, in 1951, was called 'Nefertiti Lived Here.' And it was from that fifteen-minute talk that I developed this book, first published in 1954.

It is good to know that people of an even younger generation are again coming with me as I approach that northern headland, which seemed to have slipped for ever across my last actual view of Tell el Amarna so long ago. But here I am, rounding it again in the old felucca, and the beautiful inlet can be seen beyond in the evening light, with welcoming lamplit windows of the ancient house aglow.

Again, I see the six of us at work, absorbed and purposeful, sometimes frustrated, sometimes jubilant, each of us playing a part in the effort to salvage and restore a small piece of Egyptian history. It was rather like restoring a wonderful old garment, frayed here and there – even with a few bits missing – but gradually emerging as a shapely whole. But, above all, I remember that, at every turn and twist, the hard work was lightened by something that held it together, forever glinting in and out of the fabric – the golden thread of distant laughter.

Mary Chubb, 1998

Also from Libri:

CITY IN THE SAND

Mary Chubb

With new introduction by Isabel Quigly

It is 1932: after her adventures in Egypt, conjured up so memorably in *Nefertiti Lived Here*, Mary Chubb's story continues in Iraq, ancient Mesopotamia, where she joins an American team uncovering ancient Eshnunna, a vassal city of Ur.

'Delightful and beautifully written.'

The British Museum Magazine

New edition 1999 (first published 1957).
214 pp., 43 b/w photographs. Paperback: £12.95

To be published by Libri in October 2001:

JOHN PENDLEBURY, SCHOLAR-SPY

Imogen Grundon

The first biography of the charismatic archaeologist who, having excavated at Tell el Amarna and Knossos, led the Cretan resistance to the German invasion, and was shot in 1941.

THE VILLA ARIADNE

Dilys Powell

Dilys Powell's classic account of Crete, following the inhabitants of Arthur Evans's romantic house at Knossos, which became home to John Pendlebury when he was the Curator at the site, and finally to the German General Kreipe who was living there when kidnapped by Patrick Leigh Fermor and taken over the mountains to captivity.